Parenting by the Book

Parenting by the Book

A weekly portion of chinuch banim

Rosally Saltsman

TARGUM/FELDHEIM

First published 2003
Copyright © 2003 by Rosally Saltsman
ISBN 1-56871-231-6

Published by:
TARGUM PRESS, INC.
22700 W. Eleven Mile Rd.
Southfield, MI 48034
E-mail: targum@netvision.net.il
Fax: 888-298-9992
www.targum.com

Distributed by:
FELDHEIM PUBLISHERS
202 Airport Executive Park
Nanuet, NY 10954
www.feldheim.com

Printed in Israel

Rabbi Zev Leff

Rabbi of Moshav Matityahu
Rosh Hayeshiva Yeshiva Gedola Matisyahu
D. N. Modi'in 71917 Tel. (08) 976-1138 Fax. (08) 976-5326

Dear Friends,

I have had the pleasure to read the manuscript of "Parenting by the Book" by Rosally Saltsman. The authoress uses various episodes from the weekly Torah Portion to bring out various lessons in chinuch (education). Though many of the connections between the source in the Torah and the lesson derived are not the literal meaning of the Torah source, they definitely can be classified as "*drash*," a more homiletical interpretation of the source. I have found the lessons sound from a standpoint of true Torah philosophy and they are presented in a lucid, down to earth, and enjoyable format. Chinuch — educating our children properly — is one of the foundations of Judaism. The authoress strengthens and enhances this foundation with this work.

I recommend this work to all those who seek direction and inspiration regarding chinuch.

Sincerely,
With Torah blessings,

Rabbi Zev Leff

Abraham J. Twerski, M.D.

Gateway Rehabilitation Center
Moffett Run Road
Aliquippa, PA 15001

The challenges facing parents and teachers today in providing a wholesome chinuch are unprecedented. We need every bit of wisdom available to cope successfully with this formidable challenge.

Ms. Saltsman has drawn upon Torah sources, both in the parashah and in the timeless teachings of our sages, to give us additional resources for this greatest of all our responsibilities: the chinuch of our children.

Parents and teachers will find help in *Parenting by the Book*.

Sincerely,

Abraham J. Twerski, M.D.
Founder, Medical Director Emeritus

May this book serve as an ilui neshamah
for the following people:

My mother, Anna Leitman Saltsman
חנה בת קלמן
Chana bas Kalman

My father, Maurice Saltsman
משה לייזר בן ברוך
Moshe Lazar ben Baruch

My uncle, Israel Leitman
ישראל בן קלמן
Yisrael ben Kalman

Sydney Klaiman
שמעון בן שמואל
Shimon ben Shmuel

Stephen Klaiman
שמואל בן שמעון
Shmuel ben Shimon

Norman Cuttler
שמואל נטע הלוי בן לייב
Shmuel Notte HaLevi ben Leib

Shayna Chinkah Alovich
שיינע (יפה) חינקה בת אברהם אהרן
Shayna Chinkah bas Avraham Aharon

Tzippora Benkel
צפורה בת יונה
Tzippora bas Yona

Bernard Garmaise
דב בן שמעיהו
Dov ben Shmayahu

Edith Lehrer
חיה בת יוסף
Chaya bas Yossef

Naftali Lanzkron
נפתלי בן ציון בן מאיר
Naftali Ben Tzion ben Meir

Eleanor Farkas Brandt
לאה בת אברהם זאב
Leah bas Avraham Zev

Jeannette Rozenblum
יוכבד בת אברהם יצחק
Yocheved bas Avraham Yitzchak

David Aranoff

דוד בן אריה לייב הכהן

David ben Aryeh Leib HaKohen

Isaac Yodits

יצחק בן פייגע מלכה

Yitzchak ben Faige Malka

Bernardo Avraham Levin

בערל דב אברהם בן משה מאיר

Berel Dov Avraham ben Moshe Meir

Luis Levin

לייזר ברוך לואיס בן בערל דב אברהם

Lazar Baruch Luis ben Berel Dov Avraham

Tema Pninah Looban Shapiro

תמה פנינה בת זאב ואלף

Tema Pninah bas Zev Wolf

Rachel Faith ben Zev

רחל חסידה בת הרב יהושע צבי מיכל

Rachel Chassidah bas HaRav Yehoshua Tzvi Michel

And may this book serve as a zechus for am Yisrael and
help bring Hashem's mercy upon us and speed the
coming of Mashiach bimheira b'yameinu amen.

Acknowledgments

One of the first things we are taught as children is to say thank you. Although it is one of the first concepts we learn, it is one we spend a great deal of our lives trying to master with heartfelt sincerity. I admit that it is too meager an offering to all whose debt I am in, but I want to take the opportunity to thank all who helped me produce this book.

I thank *Hashem Yisbarach* for the *siyatta diShmaya* in this and all my other endeavors. I hope that I have shown that His trust in my efforts are justified.

I offer sincere thanks and appreciation to Rav Zev Leff, Rabbi Abraham Twerski, and Dr. Miriam Adahan for reading my manuscript, offering comments and suggestions, and endorsing it as worthy of reading. I am especially grateful to Rav Leff for supplying me with the sources that I couldn't find.

I am grateful to have the honor of being inspired by Rabbi Paysach Krohn who gives selflessly of his time which is so valuable and his deep insights and positivity which is even more valuable. This book is only one of the many efforts in serving Hashem that he has inspired in me, and I am truly grateful to count myself among those whose lives he enriches.

I thank the dedicated and creatively prolific staff at Targum, led by Rabbi and Rebbetzin Dombey, Miriam Zakon, and their graphic artist, D. Liff, whose beautiful artwork makes one want to write books to do it justice. I also want to take the opportunity to thank Suri Brand and Ita Olesker for their expertise and savvy editing of my books.

My deep gratitude to my paragon of growth Rochel Bryna Frumin and her disciples, who are my friends and teachers.

To all the people who have contributed to this book I am truly thankful. To all my very special friends, I could do nothing without you.

Thanks to my two beautiful soul sisters Leah Cohen and Eva Meyer. Special thanks to Hanoch Levin. My appreciation to Amy Greenbaum Kohn and Ronni Kives.

Bea Rosenblum, your wisdom and encouragement are indefatigable.

I hope that I live up to my aspirations to be a good parent to my son, Joshua (Yehoshua Yisrael). I am grateful that Hashem has sent me such a wonderful and understanding son, *bli ayin hara*. I have learned much because of him but have learned more from him. Josh, I dedicate this book, as everything else, to you, and I hope that I merit to see you become a parent and establish a *bayis ne'eman b'Yisrael*. May your future children bring as much happiness and *nachas* to you as you have brought to me.

To parents and educators everywhere, let us create a circle of love for God, His Torah, and our families in the hearts of our children, and let our love be a link from generation to generation. From the generations that have preceded me and for the generations to follow, our greatest treasure is our living Torah scrolls, our children. May we raise our children and grandchildren in good physical, spiritual, and emotional health till 120! And may we see the coming of Mashiach with our families around us.

Contents

There are three partners in [the creation of] man:
HaKadosh Baruch Hu, his father, and his mother.

(Kiddushin 30b)

חנוך לנער על פי דרכו....
Educate a child according to his way....

(Mishlei 22:6)

Hashem gives the child his temperament and personality and abilities that the child will need in serving Him. It is up to the parents to "educate the child according to his way...."

Introduction

We must recognize that the Torah's positive messages must be transmitted at the earliest stages of life. *Chinuch* begins from the day a child is born. It is never too early to start educating children on their level.

Indeed, there is a correlation between the word חנוך, education, and the word חנוכה. A significant part of the Chanukah celebration was that the Chashmonaim reinaugurated the use of the Beis HaMikdash. Jews were free to worship Hashem, and Torah could be learned without disruption. Authentic *chinuch* could be taught.... Hence, Chanukah meant the availability of *chinuch*. And just as a *chanukas habayis* (the inauguration of a new home) is done with excitement and enthusiasm, so too the *chinuch* of children should be practiced with excitement and enthusiasm.

(*Rabbi Paysach J. Krohn,*
Reflections of the Maggid, pp. 234–35)

There is no more rewarding or gratifying job than being a parent. As parents, we emulate God by constantly giving. We serve as the guardians and guides of the precious souls of our children. We teach and nurture these souls to become God-fearing and God-serving Jews.

Chinuch is really the cornerstone of the Jewish people. Everything is built around it.

The paramount importance of *chinuch* is reflected in how it is alluded to in every parashah of the Torah. As the answers to all our questions can be found in the Torah, the answers to questions about child-rearing can be found there as well. It is my intent, *b'ezras Hashem*, to highlight the lessons presented in each parashah of the Torah for raising spiritually and emotionally healthy children.

The idea for this book came to me at a lecture on *chinuch* given by Rabbi Paysach Krohn in Beit Shemesh. Very few of these ideas are my own. They can be found in the Torah and Talmud and are cited in many of the books on the reading list at the back of this book. For reasons of simplicity, I will be using the pronouns *he* and *his* throughout the book even though I refer to both genders. Along with the books listed at the end of the book, a great many of the references and quotations have been taken from the Stone edition of the ArtScroll *Chumash*, published by Mesorah Publications.

There are a number of ideas in this book that are repeated several times. Although many books on child-rearing, including this one, may cover the same points, they bear repeating. This is because references to these appear repeatedly in the Torah, which only underscores their importance.

It is important to consider them from every angle and study and review them diligently so that thoughtful parenting becomes second nature. These ideas are offered with love and concern for the future generations of our people and for their parents who wish to raise their children according to the insights and guidelines provided by the ultimate textbook on child-rearing — the Torah.

Much of modern technology and values have dulled our naturally healthy instincts. We must relearn things that should be second nature to us, like showing affection to our children and spending quantity as well as quality time with them. We must also learn to avoid the pitfalls of previous generations and internalize the lessons taught to us through our matriarchs, patriarchs, and Torah leaders.

It is important to have a guide and a *rav* to consult with in all matters of *chinuch* and to use other parents as a resource for support, reassurance, a shoulder to cry on, a good laugh, whatever helps us keep our sanity while doing the most important job in the world — building the Jewish nation with wisdom and love.

May we all merit to build a *bayis ne'eman b'Yisrael*, raise our children to Torah, *chuppah*, and *ma'asim tovim*, and watch them become parents in good health with happiness and success until 120.

BEREISHIS

אם הבנים שמחה הללוי-ה.
Happy is the mother of children. *Halleluyah!*
(*Tehillim 113:9*)

Bereishis

In the beginning...

(Bereishis 1:1)

God created a man and a woman. Then He made them parents, and they became a mother and a father. They weren't in paradise long, but Adam and Chavah realized that by giving them children, God had given them the whole world.

God saw that the light was good, and God separated between the light and the darkness.

(Bereishis 1:4)

Everyone is made up of darkness and light; each person has both good traits and bad traits. It's important that we know how to differentiate between these traits. Rav Yerucham Levovitz, *zt"l*, says: "Woe to he who doesn't know his weaknesses, but double woe to he who doesn't know his strengths" (quoted in *Sidras Tikun HaMiddos*, "*L'Anavim Yitein Chein*," p. 164). As parents, it is our duty to make sure that our children are aware of their good traits and their bad traits, their virtues and their faults, the gifts they have to give to the world and the areas where they have to improve. Woe to the parent who doesn't know how to distinguish between the two, who thinks his child is all good or all bad. Each child is a vessel for divine light, and it is our mission to point out that special light that shines in each of our children and to teach them how to use it to illuminate the world.

God separated the light from the darkness. We need to protect our children from the darker elements. Not only from the darker side of life — the evil that lurks beyond the sanctity and safety of our homes — but from the darker sides of their parents and siblings, their own negativity, and certainly any friends or neighbors, even teachers, who pose a physical, spiritual, or emotional threat to them. A child is like a candle. We have to protect his sensitive light from the elements that are in danger of extinguishing it.

So God...separated between the waters which were beneath the firmament and the waters that were above the firmament.

(Bereishis 1:7)

A person's nature could be likened to water. God saw that one type of water is different from another, and He put each type of water in completely different places. Many parents place their children in the same environment even though they may be as different from each other as Heaven and Earth. Both the sky and the earth are essential for creation, but if we turned them around, the world as we know it would cease to exist.

One type of school may be good for one child, but it will mean spiritual decay for another. Each child needs an environment that is nurturing for his growth. Some children need intense study, the esoteric, the world of ideas, in order to thrive, and others need to be more down-to-earth, to study something more practical, more relevant for day-to-day affairs. Some need a combination of both. The same way a person who rises above a certain altitude needs oxygen to breathe because he can't adapt to the atmosphere, everyone needs to be where he can breathe easily and not feel like a fish out of water.

...fruit trees yielding fruit each after its kind.

(Bereishis 1:10)

There's a famous expression, "A fruit doesn't fall far from the tree." This means that we can't expect to raise children who are very different from ourselves, as it is written, "Succeeding your fathers will be your sons" (*Tehillim* 45:17).

If a child has a character trait or a value we like, it is quite likely he inherited it from us. Likewise, if he has a character trait we dislike, it is very likely that we are at the root of the problem.

Hashem God planted a garden in Eden, to the east, and placed there the man whom he had formed.

(Bereishis 2:8)

Adam's first home was Gan Eden. Every child's first environment should feel like paradise to him, where all his physical needs are met and he feels like the center of the universe. If he is properly nourished and feels surrounded by love, if the atmosphere is comfortable and makes him feel safe, then when he has to leave the paradise of his familial home, he'll feel better able to cope in the world. As much as possible we must make our homes into places that are child-friendly and not make our children feel lost in the woods.

Of every tree of the garden you may freely eat, but of the tree of knowledge of good and evil, you must not

eat thereof, for on the day you eat of it, you shall surely die.

(Bereishis 2:16)

Children need rules. But the rules should be there to protect them and make them into better people, not so that parents have an easier life or are able to control their children. We learn two things about discipline from the verse. God let Adam have free rein in the garden. He had only one rule: don't eat from the tree of knowledge.

Homes should not be a place that is full of limitations, restrictions, and nos. A religious child has enough restrictions and demands for self-control. Adam had a garden full of yeses and only one no. Our homes should have a similar ratio, hundreds of yeses and only a handful of nos.

The other lesson we gain from the verse is that we should have a good reason for saying no to a child — something that poses a real danger to his physical, emotional, or spiritual welfare (or someone else's) should definitely be out of bounds. Let's face it: dirt is not dangerous. Neither is staying up late occasionally, eating potato chips for dinner once in a while, falling asleep in your clothes on Shabbos, or fingering an expensive vase. These things can have unpleasant consequences at the worst. At the very least, they may be irritating to parents, but they are a far cry from peril.

> The ideal education builds children with good habits while planting in them virtuous values and perspectives.
>
> *(Lawrence Keleman, To Kindle a Soul, p. 39)*

We need to be able to differentiate between danger and inconvenience and make sure that our children's homes aren't a danger zone, or they'll go into the real world with an inappropriate perception of what is and what isn't dangerous and forbidden, and that really can be life-threatening.

Now Hashem God had formed out of the ground every beast of the field and every bird of the sky and brought them to the man to see what he would call each one; and whatever the man called each living creature, that remained its name.

(*Bereishis 2:19*)

One of our first jobs as parents is to name our progeny. This name stays with them for their entire lives. A person's name contains his essence, and parents have divine assistance in choosing a name for their child (Rav Yitzchak Luria, the Arizal, *Sefer HaGilgulim*, ch. 59). Shakespeare was wrong. There *is* a lot to a name; a name defines a person and is identified with him.

Some name their child after grandparents or other relatives; often parents just pick a name they like. Some pick traditional names, while others choose what's popular at the time. Before you name your child, give careful thought to what you want him to be, the character traits you want him to embody, and the sounds and meanings you want your child to be identified with.

Therefore a man shall leave his father and his mother and cling to his wife, and they shall become one flesh.

(*Bereishis 2:24*)

Family unity begins with the parents. Although parents can have different personalities, different interests, and different opinions, children have to feel that their parents are bound together as one loving unit. If each parent has different rules, or the parents argue with each other openly in front of their children, this causes a tense, hostile environment and causes the children to feel fearful and insecure.

This doesn't mean that parents can't disagree, but not in front of their children. Certainly they should not contradict each other.

If a child speaks disrespectfully to a parent, the other parent must feel the insult as if it were against him and should calmly but seriously tell the child that he must show deference to the other parent.

Parents, more than not disagreeing in front of their children, must express love to one another by smiling at each other, looking warmly and lovingly at one another, expressing appreciation, telling nice stories to their children about each other, and showing concern, respect, and consideration. If parents want respect and appreciation from their children, they must give it to each other. The parents are the roots of the family tree. Roots are joined to one another at the base.

Hashem God called out to the man and said to him, "Where are you?"

(Bereishis 3:11)

This and the verses that follow are a list of questions God poses to Adam and Chavah. Now we all know that God had no need to ask any of these questions; He knew the answers already. *Midrash Aggadah* says that God didn't want to terrify Adam by coming upon him suddenly and accusing him. He wanted to give Adam a chance to confess and repent. God used the same approach with Chavah (*Seforno*).

What does this teach us? Sometimes when we catch a child doing something wrong, the terror we elicit from a child who is caught is worse than the punishment he gets for the misdeed. Parents can terrify their children with an extreme reaction to a mistake the child has made. In the *Kitzur Shulchan Aruch* (165:7), it says that a child must be punished immediately for a transgression. Otherwise, he can be seriously affected by the fear of waiting. When a child does something wrong, we can emulate Hashem by approaching him calmly and quietly and eliciting information by asking questions. This gives the child a chance to own up to what he's done and gives him the feeling we are willing to listen to his side of the story. This will make him more willing to open up to us in the future.

Moreover, we are not omniscient and omnipotent like God is, and we may have misinterpreted the situation or the severity of it. By calmly going on a fact-finding mission, we can save face by not accusing a child falsely before we have all the facts.

In pain shall you bear children.

(Bereishis 3:16)

Tza'ar gidul banim is a well-known description for not only bearing children but bringing them up. God actually did parents a favor by forewarning them of what lies ahead. Parents, especially young parents, enter parenthood without really knowing what to expect. No matter how many siblings you may have, no matter how many hours of babysitting you've chalked up, it's a whole other ballgame when you have the sole responsibility for your own children and you don't have the advantage of time limitation or objective distance.

The physical exhaustion and emotional stress of child-rearing is usually greater than one could ever imagine. Forewarned is forearmed. If we know beforehand that child-rearing is going to be demanding, we have less of a chance of falling victim to unrealistic expectations we may have of ourselves and our children, and then we may be pleasantly surprised when occasionally it's not as hard as we thought.

The man called his wife's name Chavah, because she had become the mother of all the living.

(Bereishis 3:20)

Adam was named by God after the place from which he had come, the earth. Adam named Chavah based on where she was going: she would be the progenitor of all who came after her. It says in *Eishes Chayil* that an accomplished woman "anticipates the ways of her household" (*Mishlei* 31:27). Women also have *binah yeseirah*, additional insight, a unique attribute that helps them be successful mothers.

How one raises his children determines not only how his children will turn out but will also have an effect on his grandchildren and great-grandchildren. It says in *Pirkei Avos* that a wise person considers the consequences of his actions. Parents always have to keep in mind that the parenting decisions they make today affect generations of children to come, and the consequences increase exponentially like ripples in a pond. Good parenting requires forethought. While sometimes spontaneity is good, decisions whose import affects people's entire lifetimes require due deliberation.

Another interpretation of Chavah's name is that she was the mother of all the living. Some of us are lucky to have children who more than meet our expectations. *Baruch Hashem*, they're healthy and bright and bring us *nachas* in many areas. Some children are more challenging. They may have been born with a physical difficulty or emotional problem that requires more than the usual dedication and patience. There are also children who

are more difficult to love than others because of their tempera-
ments.

But mothers are required to be the mothers of "all the living."
Every child has a God-given right to physical and emotional nurturing. It is incumbent on the parents to provide that for their
children. If this proves too difficult, they must see to it that the
child is provided for by someone who can more easily care for
him.

In families where the differences between the children are
more subtle, no child should have to feel that his sibling is the favorite and that he is not as loved or appreciated. We have to
mother (and father) all of our children, not just the ones who
meet our highest expectations.

In *Don't Look Down* (pp. 115–16, published by ArtScroll),
Rabbi Michael Haber writes the following story:

> In 1989, a powerful earthquake shook Armenia. There was
> enormous loss of life. One man's experience in that event un-
> folded, more or less, in the following fashion.
>
> The man had taken his young son to school that morning.
> Now, following the earthquake, he feared for the safety of
> that son. The father ran to the school and was horrified by
> what he saw. The tremor had leveled the school. The building
> had collapsed. The man thought of his son. He recalled tuck-
> ing him into bed each evening with the words "No matter
> what, I'll always be there for you."
>
> Now the father ran to the site where his son's classroom
> had been. There was a pile of debris. He began to dig, remov-
> ing stone after stone. He asked for help from others, who re-
> fused. Nevertheless, the man continued to dig — through the
> night, through the rain. Twelve hours, twenty-four, thirty-six.
>
> In the thirty-eighth hour, he heard a voice.

"Dad, is that you? The collapsed stones formed a wedge, which kept us safe. Dad, I told my friends that you would come for me if you were alive. And I told them that when you saved me, you would save them, too. I knew that no matter what you would be there for me."

Each of our children should hold the belief in his heart that, no matter what, their parents will be there for them.

I have acquired a child with God.

(Bereishis 4:1)

According to the Ramban, Adam and Chavah realized they were mortal and that their lives on earth were limited. After giving birth to a child, Chavah said, "I have acquired a child from God to replace me and continue to serve Him when I am no longer living." A child is a divine gift who is meant to live a life that is a gift to God (*Positive Parenting*, p. 60).

When Kayin killed Hevel, history's first tragic result of sibling rivalry, God once again approached the wrongdoer with a question. He asked Kayin, "Where is Hevel your brother?" (*Bereishis* 4:9).

"And he said, 'I do not know. Am I my brother's keeper?' " (ibid.). This is a very good example of how we are role models for our children. According to Rashi, the birth of Kayin occurred before Adam and Chavah's sin and their expulsion from Gan Eden. Kayin witnessed the sin and the expulsion. He would also have witnessed his father's answer to God when He questioned him about eating from the tree: "The woman whom You gave to be with me, she gave me of the tree, and I ate" (*Bereishis* 3:12). Like father, like son. Adam didn't want to take responsibility for his actions, and, not surprisingly, neither did Kayin.

"In order to serve as proper examples for our children, we

must cleanse ourselves of every trait we would find undesirable in them" (*The Eternal Jewish Home*, p. 34). We cannot expect more from our children than we model for them with our own behavior. However, if we are lucky enough to have children who surpass us in a certain *middah*, we must acknowledge this improvement and strive to emulate them.

The Midrash relates that when Adam asked Kayin what had happened to God's judgment against him, he answered that he had repented and was granted mercy. Adam then realized the power of *teshuvah* and composed psalm 92 in honor of Shabbos (Rebbetzin Esther Jungreis, *A Committed Life*, p. 287).

Adam learned about repentance from his son. There are things we can all learn from our children. And admitting this makes our lessons to them easier to swallow.

Noach

These are the offspring of Noach — Noach was a righteous man, perfect in his generations; Noach walked with God. Noach had begotten three sons: Shem, Cham, and Yefes.

(Bereishis 6:9–10)

The Radak says that the Torah mentions Noach's children after his righteousness to indicate that he instilled such behavior into his children. This shows that you have to strive to perfect yourself before you can hope to perfect your children.

Noach had begotten three sons: Shem, Cham, and Yefes.

(Bereishis 6:10)

According to the Talmud (*Sanhedrin* 69b), the order of birth of the sons was Yefes, Cham, and Shem. Shem was the youngest, but he had the most wisdom. He was the progenitor of Avraham Avinu, whose grandson went to learn in the yeshivah that Shem founded with his great-grandson Ever.

One lesson this teaches us is that we should learn with our children. Shem learned with his grandson, and Ever learned with his great-great-grandson. We should study not only with our sons and fathers, but also with our grandfathers and grandchildren.

> In choosing which languages to speak with the child, one should consider also the language of the grandparents, for they will thereby gain much pleasure from their grandchildren and can also teach them their qualities.
>
> *(The Eternal Jewish Home, p. 135)*

Children, parents, and grandparents may all have been born in different countries and have different mother tongues. In order to learn with each other, they must all be able to communicate. Therefore it is necessary that they learn to speak the same language both figuratively and literally. As an aside, it's a good idea for children to learn more than one language. Studies show that this increases brain mass and, by definition, intelligence, and of course all Jewish children should learn Hebrew.

Yefes personifies beauty, Cham, emotions, and Shem, identity and self-knowledge. These three names signify the attributes a parent should instill in his children: a sense of identity that is linked to the soul (the name Shem contains the inner letters of the Hebrew word *neshamah*, soul); aesthetic appreciation, the infrastructure of the world; and how to channel one's energy (the name Cham means "heat"), inner drives, and emotions (Rabbi Shamshon Raphael Hirsh in the name of the Maharal of Prague).

As we instill these qualities in our children, we must remember that the emotions are subservient to the aesthetic and both are subservient to the soul. When developing these character traits in our children, we must keep our priorities straight. A Jewish education and refinement of the soul takes precedence over art lessons and gymnastics, which all take precedence over trips to the amusement park. They are all necessary — in the right proportion.

At the end of the parashah, Cham discovers his father, Noach, naked and inebriated. Cham tells his two brothers, who cover him, Yefes while looking at him and Shem avoiding seeing his father in that state. This sequence of events illustrates that while we must instill in our children each of the qualities that Noach's sons personified, the percentages of the characteristics should not be equal. The emotional element should be the least part of a person, or it can lead to impetuous and shameful behavior as Cham demonstrated. While aesthetics are important, there is a time and a place for everything. Propriety should dictate when the body should be appreciated and when it should be ignored. Shem, having a full sense of his identity and what that entailed — modesty and righteousness — was the only one of his brothers who was able to look away and concentrate on the task at hand, which was preserving the dignity of his father.

The order of Noach's children's births underscores another point. It is only as we mature that we understand what has true significance and eternal meaning. When we are young, we value what is beautiful and pleasing to the eye. As we get older, we follow our hearts and invest our emotions in causes and relationships. It is only when we mature that we discover who we truly are, and that is when we focus more on our spiritual development.

As parents, it is also important that we keep in mind the various stages our children go through as they grow. Our parenting skills, the teaching techniques we use to guide them, and our expectations should be age appropriate. While we should not encourage vanity or excessive emotionality in our children, we need to understand that it's a young girl's nature to be preoccupied with how she looks. It's logical that this preoccupation occurs when she's a teenager, which corresponds to the time that she is going to be starting to think about looking for a *shidduch*. (This phenomenon occurs in young men as well.)

A young man who gets emotionally involved with causes and finding his path in life is doing what he is supposed to be doing as a young man. This also, by the way, helps in his finding a *shidduch*. Once the eyes and the heart have been satiated, a person can start perfecting his character and building his home and his destiny.

Warning: Adolescence is a time when many children go through a second infancy. They spend a lot of time eating and sleeping. Parents who are not forearmed with this knowledge may think that their child is lazy, ungrateful for the food he has, or gluttonous. But what appears to be overeating and sleeping too much is the adolescent body's way of storing energy for a growth spurt unparalleled since infancy.

You cannot ignore the extensive and rapid physical and emotional changes that occur in teenagers. The same way parents tell themselves, "It's a developmental stage," when children exhibit this behavior at two, they should repeat the mantra now.

Eating and sleeping a lot as well as moodiness and oversensitivity are *normal* behaviors of an adolescent. Adolescence is also one of the first times you get feedback on how you're doing as a parent. The better the relationship that you have built with your child, the better you'll both weather this stage. If, despite your preparation and this awareness, it's worse than you thought, it might be a good time to consult with an expert.

As in all stages of development, the experts advise that one avoid confrontations and power struggles and not treat every occurrence of apparent disrespect or infraction of rules as a tragedy or potential tragedy.

A window shall you make for the ark.

(Bereishis 6:16)

The Torah calls this window a *tzohar*. *Tzohar* means "illumination." *Teivah*, ark, can also mean a letter of the alphabet. This teaches that we should illuminate our speech (*No'am Elimelech, Noach*). What does it mean to illuminate our speech? It can mean many things — that our speech be clear and unambiguous, that our speech be positive and full of emotional light, that our speech be enlightening and inspiring.

While it's difficult for each and every one of our utterances to answer all this lofty criteria, we can use it as a guideline to ensure that when we speak to our children we make our meaning clear, that we speak positively rather than negatively, and that we use opportunities of discourse to inspire and not degrade. Light is pure. Our speech must be the same.

And from all that lives, of all flesh, two of each shall you bring into the ark to keep alive with you; they shall be male and female.

(Bereishis 6:19)

We can learn from here a lesson in parenting. While the ideal is, of course, that both parents raise their child, today's high incidence of divorce and other tragedies, *Rachmana litzlan*, have resulted in many single-parent families. It is important that both the mother and the father be involved in raising their children. This is vital even if the parents are divorced. When one of the parents is unavailable or if, *Rachmana litzlan*, one parent has died, the other parent should seek a surrogate as a role model. This could be a grandparent, aunt or uncle, rabbi or *rebbetzin*, or a good friend.

Then Hashem said to Noach, "Come to the ark, you
and all your household."

(Bereishis 7:1)

God could have decided to save only Noach and his wife, but
He told Noach to bring their children and their children's wives,
too. Family togetherness is important, not only when there's a
deluge. Years ago people lived in extended families. At the very
most, they lived a few doors away from their married children. It
was not uncommon for grandparents, aunts, uncles, and cousins to live in the same neighborhood for decades.

Now it's hard to get them on the cell phone if you're lucky
enough to live within calling distance. Families live far from one
another and getting them together involves months of planning
and very often trans-Atlantic phone calls. While travel may be
relatively easy and flying is frequent, this doesn't take the place
of weekly family dinners, growing up with your cousins, or just
hanging around at your relatives' homes. Therefore, the influence of older family members is greatly restricted.

The frenetic pace of life also means that parents and children
spend less time together. Even when they do take vacations,
many parents take holidays away from their children. This is no
way to build family unity, harmony, or traditions.

My best friend's grandfather, Yitzchak Yoditz, z"l, passed
away at the age of ninety-two. Zeide Isaac, as everyone called
him, was very much a part of his family's life and spent
Shabbosos and holidays with them.

My friend's brother, Ralph Cohen, delivered the eulogy at the
funeral in Montreal. This is what he said:

"Thank you all for coming to pay tribute to my *zeide*. My *zeide*
was a great man. I had the privilege of living with him for three
years. Every week I would get a lecture from him about life, mo-

rality, and philosophy in my younger years, and later on in life he would speak to me about marriage, relationships, and conflict resolution. Every time I would come to him to complain about someone, his answer was always the same: 'He said, she said, you said, I said... I don't want to hear any gossip! I didn't gossip with your *bubby*. I never liked to gossip with anyone. You have to find out what the real problem is.'

" 'You don't know people,' he would tell me. 'You don't know what they've been through. *Adam karov l'atzmo.*'

"My *zeide* may have been a scholar, a consummate intellectual, but his rules for living were simple. *Shvil hazahav*, the golden path, he used to say. Everything in moderation. He was a great admirer of Maimonides and must have read *Mishnah Torah* over a hundred times. These were the precepts that my *zeide* lived by. My *zeide* practiced what he preached — never a harsh word without a reason, even when he was angry, always giving people the benefit of the doubt. He was the personification of *chesed*, kindness.

"Everyone who knew my grandfather knew that there was something special about him. His neighbors admired him. He inspired young people he met in the street to go to school and learn a trade. My *zeide* was so popular that sometimes I felt like I was living with a celebrity. Whenever I walked with him, I felt that I was basking in an aura of beautiful, soft yellow light. This must be what they call *ohr tzaddik*, the light of the tzaddik. That was my *zeide*."

A child who grows up basking in the light of his grandfather's influence becomes an adult who has internalized the values he so admired in his grandfather. These values can't be learned long distance.

How many children today have frequent access to the love and wisdom of their grandparents? The support of a family system has never been more important. The more time families spend with each other the better. It's imperative that at least the immediate family (parents and children) make time to be together at least one day or evening a week.

Shabbos is an opportune time for families to spend together, but there are usually commitments such as *shiurim* and *Tehillim* groups, youth groups or other activities, and many families have guests for at least part of the time. Togetherness is something that must be worked on, but it is essential for fostering the love, bonding, and quality time necessary for raising secure and happy children.

> Studies of adolescents and young adults, as well as of school-children of different ages from nursery school up, [indicate] that those who are most emotionally stable and make the most of their opportunities are those who have parents who, whilst always encouraging their children's autonomy, are nonetheless available and responsive when called upon. Unfortunately, of course, the reverse is also true.
>
> (Bowlby, *Secure Base*, p. 124, quoted in *To Kindle a Soul*, p. 105)

Of the clean animal, of the animal that is not clean.

(*Bereishis 7:8*)

God uses the phrase "*einenah tehorah* — that is not clean," rather than "*temei'ah* — unclean." It is a fine line, but it makes a difference in our perception. Perhaps we can learn from this that even if someone has a partiality to one of his children or students, he should never show it directly. If for some reason we have to mention how a child is better at something than another child, it would be best to cushion our words and deemphasize the difference.

So he put forth his hand and took it and brought it to
him to the ark.

(Bereishis 8:9)

Noach sent the dove out three times to see if the waters had
subsided enough that he could leave the ark. The first time the
dove returned, and Noach stretched out his arm and took it back
into the ark. The second time the dove returned with an olive
branch, and the third time it did not return at all.

I think this is a wonderful metaphor for children leaving the
nest. Children begin the process of leaving home very early. At
first they don't go very far and eagerly return to our outstretched
arms. Then they begin going out into the world to school, to
camp, to friends, and they return with souvenirs of their adven-
tures — things they bought or found or received as presents.
Finally they leave home, never to return except to visit, hopefully
frequently, as they start building their own homes and raising
their own children.

Children need to feel that they have a loving home to return
to and that their parents will be there waiting for them. Young
children automatically hold out their arms when they see their
parents. Parents should greet their children with outstretched
arms, waiting to take them back into the safety and familiarity of
their homes. When children come home, parents shouldn't be in
another room or talking on the phone; they should be ready and
waiting for them, scanning the horizons, looking forward to seeing them, just as Noach waited for the dove. If the parent can't be
there, someone else should be waiting for them. The mother can
leave a note or a small treat, and she should call to welcome her
child home from wherever she is. That way the child will feel that
his parents care enough about him to make sure he got home
safely and to ask about his day.

It's a lonely feeling to come home to an empty house. Even an older child feels better knowing someone is waiting for him, even if it's a friend or a babysitter.

When children start bringing parts of the outside world home with them, they are bringing something that is important to them. The olive branch was important to the dove, so that's what she brought to Noach.

The olive branch is a symbol of peace. If you want peace with your children, respect what's important to them. If they bring home artwork, hang it on the fridge, admire it, frame it, display it. Don't throw it away or relegate it to a desk drawer. A child's rock collection is like a fine-art collection to an art patron. Sticky slimy things and junk picked up off the street are your child's discoveries. Within reason, let him keep them at least for a few days.

> Children, like most other people, identify with their own spe-
> cific interests. As adults, we usually associate ourselves
> closely with the things that are important to us.... If we have a
> hobby or favorite pastime, we naturally feel an affinity to-
> ward anyone who shares the same interest.... It boosts the
> child's self-esteem immeasurably if parents take a genuine
> interest in all that is important to the child. This is so because
> the message to the child is "I care so much about you that any-
> thing or anyone who is important to you is something or
> someone whom I want to get to know better."
>
> (*Partners with Hashem, p. 32*)

You may not be familiar with the Digimons — digital mon-sters who hook up to a child destined to help them save the world from evil. My son was very into them and collected their cards. There are dozens of Digimon monsters, and I couldn't re-member their names, which frustrated my son no end. So I memorized them, sixty or seventy three- to four-syllable names with only minor mnemonic clues to help me. We would sit together, and he would test me, delighted when I would remember them and undoubtedly feeling superior when I did not. Now he memorizes *mishnayos*. And he still has the advantage on me.

We regard many of children's passing — and not so passing — interests as silly or trivial, but since it's important to them, we should make it important to us. Then the child sees himself as important to us (which he is).

As children get older, they develop their own taste in games, music, and *objets d'art* for their rooms. It's your child's room. Let him express himself as much as possible in his choice of décor so long as he doesn't violate any basic tenets of the *chinuch* you're trying to instill in him.

When the time comes for children to leave the nest, we have to let them fly. Parenting, if done well, is a job that you work yourself out of. All the practice flights have been leading up to this. If you've done a good job, your child will still keep you on as a consultant.

And you be fruitful and multiply.

(Bereishis 9:7)

God repeats this command several times in the first chapters of *Bereishis*. While large families may present many challenges, there are also many joys to be found. In my own personal experience, I have never heard either the parents or children of such families complain; quite the contrary.

During *birkas kohanim*, a father wraps his tallis over his children. A man is said to resemble an angel when he wears his tallis. During *birkas kohanim* he looks like an angel spreading his wings protectively over little cherubs. The more children a man has, the more he has to spread his arms out to encircle them. The more children, the greater the wingspan and the higher he can fly.

People who regard children as inconvenient are missing the point. It's true that children are a big responsibility and require emotional, physical, and economic investment. But the joys far outweigh the trials and tribulations, and God provides the ideal situation for each soul that comes into the world. Every Friday night we bless each of our children. Each one adds a blessing.

> ## This is the sign of the covenant that I have confirmed between Me and all flesh that is upon the earth.
>
> *(Bereishis 9:17)*

God made a promise to Noach that he would not bring another flood upon the earth. He then placed a rainbow in the sky that would appear when it rained as a reminder of His promise.

It seems unnecessary for God to provide a guarantee that He will keep his promise — not only a guarantee but one that will always be visible and recur forever. The truth is, whenever God makes a promise, He accompanies it with a sign. Why is this necessary?

To God, a promise is very serious. That's why, when we say we're going to do something, we always add "*bli neder*" or "*b'ezras Hashem*." We're not meant to make promises we can't keep.

When we make promises to our children, we have to make sure that we carry them out (*Sukkah* 46b). If we fail to keep our promises, we are not only disappointing our children; we are teaching them to lie and to mistrust us. If we want our children to do what we say, *we* have to do what we say, and if we can accompany our promises with tangible proof (having tickets to an event, letting them hear us clearing our schedule, packing a bag for the beach), all the better.

Cham, the father of Canaan, saw his father's nakedness and told his two brothers outside.

(Bereishis 9:22)

It's interesting that in the ark, where the families lived in close proximity and there was a greater chance of being seen in an immodest state, this event didn't transpire. Noach was seen by his son only after he let his morality lapse and got drunk.

As parents, we are paragons for our children. We are walking, talking embodiments of the values we want our children to internalize. We can't afford to be caught off guard. Of course, we are human, and since our children live with us under the same roof, they are going to see us at our worst sometimes. But we have to make sure that we don't put ourselves in situations where we are ripe for a fall.

Cursed is Canaan; a slave of slaves shall he be to his brothers.

(Bereishis 9:25)

Noach curses Canaan, Cham's son. Why didn't he curse Cham? Cham was the one who had behaved disrespectfully toward his father.

Noach knew that our actions determine what our children become. Noach cursed Canaan, because he knew that if Cham could behave that way, his children would follow his example.

Rabbi Abraham Twerski writes that a person's first connection with his self is through his body. Therefore parents must never react to any part of their child's body or bodily functions with disgust or discourage children from taking pride in their bodies and what they are capable of doing. However, Jewish law requires modesty to be instilled at a young age. The best way to do this is to emphasize how beautiful and precious the child's body is and therefore it must be hidden from view, the same way a precious jewel is kept in a velvet box.

A person must love his physical self as well as his spiritual and emotional self. Sensitivity must be used in teaching modesty so that we don't teach our children to feel aversion for their bodies.

Lech Lecha

Go yourself from your land.... And I will make you a
great nation.

(Bereishis 12:1–2)

According to Rashi, Avraham would not merit children
where he was, in Ur Kasdim. It was only in Canaan where he
would merit having children. Many of us live in areas that are
fine to live in when we're single, but these places are not condu-
cive to raising children. Children need to be in a place where
there are good schools, parks where they can play safely, activities that bolster their physical and spiritual development, and
plenty of children their own age. Parents themselves need a support system; they cannot live in a spiritual wasteland where the
community isn't set up for family life.

Our first role as parents is to make sure we live in a setting
that is beneficial for family life even if that involves a move —
even a move away from family. God tells Avraham that He is going to make him into a great nation. It is for his future descendants, his children, that Avraham leaves his home and moves to
Canaan.

We are living at a time when there are many *ba'alei teshuvah*
whose commitment to a new way of life forces them to leave their

families and their families' influence in a way that parallels Avraham Avinu's journey. Often this involves a great deal of friction, discomfort, and sacrifice. But it is for the sake of the next generation, their future descendants, that they do this.

And Avraham threw himself upon his face and laughed.

(Bereishis 17:17)

Both Onkelos and Rashi interpret Avraham's laughter as joy. Here he was ninety-nine years old, and he was about to become a father for the second time, to have a son who was to be his heir.

Unlike Avraham, some people receive the news that they're going to be parents with ambivalence. Of course there's joy, but there's also fear, uncertainty, and worry. That's normal. However, the Torah tells us that the primary reaction should be one of joy, a realization that children are a blessing. Parents should be falling over themselves in appreciation to God and laughing from joy.

On that day Avraham was circumcised with Yishmael his son.

(Bereishis 17:26)

The surest way to guarantee that our children adopt our values is to serve as a role model. Whatever we want our children to do or be we need to do or be ourselves.

Ultimately, the whole educational endeavor rides on our character — on who we are and who we are willing to become.

(To Kindle a Soul, p. 194).

Avraham circumcised himself on the same day he circumcised his son. On the third day after being circumcised, Avraham ran out to greet his guests, even though he was in great pain, and then sent Yishmael, who was also in pain, to prepare the calf for the meal. Yishmael honored the guests, but only after he saw his father get up to do so. We see here that it's important for us to conduct ourselves in the way we want our children to behave, to model the behavior we want our children to emulate.

The *middos* which the tzaddik toils to acquire during his lifetime will become second nature to his children.

(Ruach Chaim, Avos 5:4)

Vayeira

And Sarah laughed at herself....

(*Bereishis* 18:12)

Simchah is a *segulah* for having children. It is written, "Happy is the mother of children" (*Tehillim* 113:9). Happiness is not only the result of having children, but it is a prerequisite, as it says (*Yeshayahu* 54:1), "Sing out, barren one, who has not given birth" (Rav Shai Zevin, *Sippurei Chassidim*).

Besides, happy parents raise happy children.

For I have loved him, because he commands his children and his household after him.

(*Bereishis* 18:19)

According to Rashi, God loved Avraham because he taught his children to follow in His ways. A person's values are revealed by what he teaches his children. And Avraham taught by example.

The people of Sedom converged on the house from young to old.

(*Bereishis* 19:4)

Here, too, is a case of teaching by example. Surely the young people of Sedom were not born cruel and inhospitable. In Sedom, the old taught the young to despise strangers. Hatred and prejudice are learned concepts. Just as Avraham taught love and charity in his home, the people of Sedom taught hatred and intolerance in theirs, and so the young converged upon the house with the old.

> I have two daughters who have never known a man. I shall bring them out to you and do to them as you please; but to these men do nothing inasmuch as they have come under the shelter of my roof.
>
> *(Bereishis 19:8)*

It's difficult to comprehend how a man who would go to such lengths to save total strangers from the perverted and angry mob would be willing to sacrifice his own daughters to it. But mixed-up priorities is not the sole domain of Lot. How many parents spend evenings and weekends at work ostensibly to give their children a better life while taking very little part in that life? How many parents put more store in what the neighbors think than in what's best for their children? Unfortunately, it is not uncommon for parents to sacrifice their children's well-being to conform to the norms and priorities of society.

> Adults who come into therapy often reveal a great deal of anger because they feel they have been "used" to satisfy parental needs.... If they are seen *primarily* as extensions of the parents rather than as independent beings, even such sacrifice is not truly altruistic.
>
> *(Positive Parenting, p. 36)*

Many parents will dedicate hours of time, tons of energy, and large sums of money to charitable causes while ostensibly not having these things for their own families. Charity begins at home, with our own children. Their welfare is paramount. According to *Midrash Tanchuma*, Lot ended up sinning with his own daughters because he was willing to have them dishonored by the mob. Also, since they had heard their father's offer of giving them into the hands of the mob, the older one was able to conceive of sinning with her father. She was just following his moral lead.

When parents think nothing of breaking rules and committing illegal acts, it is not surprising that their offspring follow in their footsteps. Both Lot and his daughter had noble intentions — his was to protect the visitors and hers to propagate humanity. But in both cases the means was far from justified.

And Avraham was a hundred years old when his son Yitzchak was born to him.

(Bereishis 21:5)

For I have borne him a child in his old age!

(Bereishis 21:7)

Avraham and Sarah are the prototype of parents who have children late in their lives. Child-rearing presents certain difficulties for parents who are not in their prime. Yet Avraham and Sarah raised a wonderful son despite this. Sarah was ninety years old when Yitzchak was born, yet she refers to the old age of Avraham. What about her old age?

A new mother, whatever her age, doesn't feel old. Tired, yes. Overwhelmed, definitely, but giving birth is rejuvenating. Mothers bring new life into the world.

Also, children keep us young because they keep us acting

young. It's hard to feel old when you're going down the slide with your toddler. Although young parents have more energy than older ones, older parents rediscover their youth. The sagacity and tranquility they have gained over the years often more than make up for their fading vigor.

The child grew and was weaned.

(Bereishis 20:8)

Jewish tradition encourages women to nurse a long time. The Talmud advises that a child should ideally nurse for two to five years, depending on his state of health (*Shulchan Aruch, Yoreh Deah* 81:7). Nursing is considered the best form of nourishment — both physical and spiritual.

> In my opinion, the most important period for education is that time when true *chinuch* is most ignored, a period of time when education is deemed not possible — the first years of a child's life — the nursing years.
>
> (Rav Shamshon Raphael Hirsch, Yesodot HaChinuch, vol. 2, pp. 44–45, quoted in Straight from the Heart, by Tehilla Abramov, p. 21)

A nursing child is being educated in love. And as he nurses, the child is absorbing his mother's words, observing her body language, and forming impressions of what love and intimacy is all about. "Perhaps it constitutes the single most attentive and affectionate act a mother can do for her infant" (*To Kindle a Soul*, p. 116).

Avraham made a great feast on the day Yitzchak was weaned. This shows us that we should express our gratitude to Hashem when He provides us with children, celebrating the milestones in their lives. We should take the opportunity to show our excitement when a child cuts a new tooth or loses one, takes his first step or his first test, gets his first report card or goes on his first *shidduch*. Firsts by definition are once-in-a-lifetime experiences.

> She went and sat herself down at a distance, some bowshots away, for she said, "Let me not see the death of the child." And she sat at a distance, lifted her voice, and wept.
>
> *(Bereishis 21:16)*

Who measures the distance of a mother to a child by bowshots? Perhaps a mother who abandons her child in his pain is compared to someone brandishing a weapon. Rav Shamshon Raphael Hirsch describes Hagar's behavior in this situation as disgraceful and selfish. Instead of comforting her son in his dying moments, she took refuge so she would not have to witness his pain. That is why, says Rav Hirsch, God hearkened to his cries and not hers. How could God turn a deaf ear, as it were, to a mother's cries for her child? Because she was really crying for her own agony, not his.

When, God forbid, our children are suffering, when they are in pain or sick, we need to comfort them and share their pain with them. A trouble shared is a trouble halved, and no one can feel our pain like our parents can. It is certainly preferable that a parent care for a sick child and not a caretaker, unless it is someone the child knows and trusts well (or, of course, if the child has a chronic illness, and there are other children to take care of or the mother herself is ill or unable to cope).

God had to tell Hagar to take Yishmael by the hand. Parents who have little choice but to relegate the care of their children to caretakers should make every effort to be with their children themselves when they are in a vulnerable state. That's when children need the comfort of their parents most. This is especially true if the reason for the parents' absence is their own discomfort or inconvenience. Many jobs allow parents to use their own sick leave to be with a sick child or to take vacation days.

It is perhaps because Hagar's distance from her son was measured in bowshots that he became an archer. Perhaps because her compassion was overshadowed by her self-interest, her son chose an occupation where compassion for life is overshadowed by self-interest.

And his mother took a wife for him from the land of Egypt.

(Bereishis 21:21)

A father has the mitzvah of finding a wife for his son. However, it is a good idea for both parents to be involved in seeking spouses for their children. Although the type of involvement may vary and may constitute only emotional support, it's good for children to know that their parents are there for them during this critical time in their lives.

Please, take your son, your only one, whom you love, Yitzchak, and go to the land of Moriah; bring him up there as an offering upon one of the mountains which I shall tell you.

(Bereishis 22:2)

Because you have done this thing and have not withheld your son, your only one, that I shall surely bless you and greatly increase your offspring.

(Bereishis 22:16–17)

According to Rav Yosef Ibn Kaspi (1279–1340), Avraham provides a lesson to all parents. Parents need to know when to let go of their children, when their children should not be expected to sacrifice themselves for their parents.

Yitzchak was thirty-seven years old at the time of the sacrifice. He was willing to offer himself up willingly, but when God said it wasn't necessary, Avraham cut him loose to study at the yeshivah of Shem and Ever (*Targum Yonasan*). *That* was the final test of Avraham.

Chayei Sarah

Hashem had blessed Avraham with everything.

(Bereishis 21:1)

"With everything" in Hebrew is בכל, which has the numerical value of fifty-two, the same numerical value as בן, son *(Akeidas Yitzchak)*. A person's children are considered everything to him. Though we tend to be preoccupied with making a living, our material possessions, and our day-to-day routine, what we treasure most is our children.

We need to remember that our children are, indeed, everything to us and make sure they know this. This also teaches them what should be important to them when they're older — their own children and not vain pursuits.

Another proof that "everything" refers to Yitzchak is that the next verse is Avraham's instruction to Eliezer to find Yitzchak a wife.

Rather, to my land and to my kindred shall you go and take a wife for Yitzchak.

(Bereishis 24:4)

Eliezer is the first matchmaker mentioned in the Torah. He

was Avraham's most trusted servant, yet Avraham made him swear that he wouldn't take a wife from among the Canaanite women.

We learn three rules related to finding a *shidduch* for our children from this verse:

1. Find a matchmaker you trust.
2. Make sure the matchmaker finds a *shidduch* with similar values to your own family.
3. Don't rush to break off a *shidduch*.

Why would Avraham need to make Eliezer swear regarding the girl he would bring home? Couldn't Avraham reject Eliezer's choice if she were not up to par?

Apparently Avraham thought that breaking off a *shidduch* was not an option and that once Eliezer had committed Avraham he would be obligated to go through with it. Although there are certainly cases when breaking off a *shidduch* is necessary, it shouldn't be taken lightly and should be done only in consultation with a Torah authority.

> And he said, "Hashem, God of my master Avraham, may You so arrange it for me this day that You do kindness with my master Avraham."
>
> (*Bereishis* 24:12)

The first thing Eliezer did when he arrived in Aram Naharayim was to pray to God for success. In any matter of child-rearing, this is the first order of business: to pray to God for success.

The test Eliezer came up with for Yitzchak's future bride involved hospitality to wayfarers. This was in keeping with Avraham's request to find someone of similar values for his son.

"Let us call the maiden and ask her decision." They called Rivkah and said to her, "Will you go with this man?"

(*Bereishis 24:57–58*)

It is significant that Rivkah's mother and brother and Eliezer decided to ask Rivkah's opinion. According to one interpretation, Rivkah was only three years old at the time since her birth is mentioned in the Torah after the *akeidah* three years earlier. Even if, according to other opinions, she was a teenager, her family didn't make a fateful decision without consulting her.

Many parents are quick to decide things that will alter their children's lives without consulting them. Decisions such as what schools they should attend, where they should live, whom they should marry, and how to spend their money are all things in which children should have a say.

It is also never too early to consult with children regarding decisions that concern them, since ultimately children are going to have to make their own decisions. Like anything else, practice makes them better at it.

Also, making decisions or even offering opinions regarding other people's decisions helps build self-esteem. Letting a child choose his clothing for the day at kindergarten or what he wants to eat for lunch or what present he'd like to buy his baby sister are all choices even toddlers are capable of making. Surely older children should be able to choose their extracurricular activities and what high school to attend. Certainly, as the verse implies, no child should be forced to do anything against his will. People are more cooperative when allowed to do things in which they have a say.

What kind of wife would Rivkah have been if she had been forced to go against her will, before she was ready? What kind of person would Rivkah have become if she had been forced to stay against her will? Her family showed wisdom in allowing her to make the decision. And surely, if Rivkah was consulted about such a weighty matter, she had already had experience making decisions.

And she said, "I will go." So they escorted Rivkah their sister and her nurse, as well as Avraham's servant and his men.

(Bereishis 24:58–59)

As the end of the story shows, Rivkah's decision to go with Eliezer was the determining factor. When we allow our children independence, we have to make sure that they are properly protected, as did Rivkah's family by sending her nurse to accompany her.

Toldos

The children agitated within her.

(Bereishis 25:22)

When Rivkah was expecting, her twin sons reacted differently to different stimuli. According to the Midrash (cited by Rashi), Yaakov became active when Rivkah would pass the Torah academy, and Esav reacted when she passed a temple of idol worship. God told her that she was to give birth to twins.

The fact that babies are influenced even before birth has been proven by scientific studies that have tested unborn children's reactions to different stimuli such as food, music, the voices of their parents, even their mothers' emotional reactions. In the first chapter of *Shoftim*, Shimshon's mother is told that she is not to eat grapes or drink wine because her child would be a *nazir* from birth. This indicates that a woman's actions can have an effect on her unborn child.

Parenthood doesn't begin at birth; it begins even before conception. Certainly the emotional, physical, and spiritual state of the mother affects her unborn children. It is important for a woman to take care of herself when she's expecting. If she eats non-kosher food, it could affect the child, as would alcohol or nicotine. It influences her child if she listens to rock music or *divrei Torah* (actually, babies like rock music, but *divrei Torah* are better for them).

It's important that a mother be in a positive frame of mind as much as possible. A fetus hears his mother praying and singing or yelling and crying. One may ask, if this is true, why did Rivkah give birth to two completely different children?

The children's reactions answer the question. Esav reacted when Rivkah passed a place of idol worship, and Yaakov reacted when she passed a *beis midrash*. One fetus integrated one type of stimuli, while the other integrated the other. While it's impossible to avoid all exposure to negative or unsavory stimuli while she's expecting, a woman has to take into consideration that she has no way of knowing how each situation will affect her baby. If she breathes both fresh air and toxic fumes, she can only hope that the fresh air will have a good effect on the baby and that somehow he will be spared the ill effects of exposure to the toxic fumes. But there's no way of knowing which will affect the child more.

While many aspects of a child's personality are divinely decreed, how these are encouraged to grow is determined by the influence of certain stimuli as early as in the womb.

The lads grew up, and Esav became one who knows hunting, a man of the field; but Yaakov was a wholesome man, abiding in tents.

(Bereishis 25:27)

Rav Hirsch writes that the essential problem with Yaakov and Esav was that they received the same treatment even though they were very different. What works well for one child may not work for the other. Had Yitzchak and Rivkah taken into account their different natures, they could have directed Esav toward mitzvos (*Yesodos HaChinuch*, vol. 1, p. 72).

Yitzchak loved Esav, for game was in his mouth; but
Rivkah loved Yaakov.

(Bereishis 25:28)

Yitzchak favored Esav, and Rivkah favored Yaakov. When
parents play favorites, it causes sibling rivalry. It is very important for a child to feel loved by both parents to the same degree as
the other children in the family. Although all children are different, and each has his own unique relationship with his parents, a
child should always be secure in the love of his parents. Parents
need to constantly work at developing a close bond with each
child, even if they have to work harder at it with some children
than with others.

When Esav was forty years old, he took as a wife
Yehudis the daughter of Be'eiri the Hittite and Basmas
the daughter of Elon the Hittite. And they were a
source of spiritual rebellion to Yitzchak and Rivkah.

(Bereishis 26:35)

The only place where Yitzchak and Rivkah were of one mind
concerning their children was when Esav took Hittite wives. The
point is emphasized by the fact that the word *haChitti*, "the
Hittite," is repeated twice in the verse. In other words, it was a
double blow. This shows how important it is for parents to show
unity. We see that by the end of the parashah, Esav went to pick a
wife from the children of Yishmael to appease his parents.

I will bless you and increase your offspring because
of Avraham My servant.

(Bereishis 26:24)

God appears to Yitzchak and reassures him that He will be with him. Why? Because of his father Avraham. Although God allots reward and punishment according to the deeds of a person, there is also the concept of *zechus avos* — the merit of our fathers is passed down to the children. When we consider performing an action, we usually only consider the ramifications it has on us in our lifetime, and then usually only on our immediate future. We need to consider, however, that if our actions have a ripple effect on the next generation, and even the generation after that, then whatever we do affects the lives of our children and grandchildren. That causes one to think twice about everything he does.

The bestowing of the blessings of Yaakov and Esav is a difficult issue that has been grappled with and discussed at length by biblical scholars throughout the generations. I wish to address only one aspect of it.

As parents, we pray to God that we should have the spiritual and physical means to bless our children with everything they need. What we also need, however, is the wisdom to know what blessings to bestow on which child. Yitzchak wanted to bestow two sets of blessings — one on each of his sons (*Seforno*). Rivkah felt that both the material and spiritual blessings should be bestowed on Yaakov, and rightly so, since she had had a prophecy to that effect when she was expecting.

Thus we should pray that we will know exactly what each child needs to actualize his potential. For some it's money, for others education, for still others moral support and guidance. In the same way that a farmer tends different crops differently, feeding, trimming, and watering each in such a way as to ensure their optimal growth, so each child needs the material, emotional, and spiritual blessings that are unique to his particular potential for growth. "Each child according to his way," as King Shlomo tells us.

But his mother said to him, "Your curse be on me, my son."

(*Bereishis 27:13*)

Ibn Ezra comments that Rivkah said this because it is the way of women to be compassionate, and they are prepared to suffer to protect their children. This is an admirable quality. A Jewish mother should be ready to sacrifice for her children. If she isn't willing to do this, she is liable to suffer the curses that may befall a person who hasn't received the proper education and guidance. In the end, Rivkah made a very big sacrifice; after sending Yaakov away, she never saw him again. By arranging that Yitzchak blessed Yaakov in place of Esav, she deprived herself of her beloved son for the rest of her life, a sacrifice of epic proportions.

Although Esav is traditionally depicted as evil, the honor he showed his father remains the paradigm of *kibbud av*. This is why he merited to receive a blessing from his father. Even if a child does something to disappoint his parents or even, God forbid, goes off the *derech*, we must give him credit for the good that he does. If Esav, who embodied evil, was held in such high esteem for his *kibbud av*, surely our children deserve to be praised for even the slightest positive behavior that they demonstrate.

Often we are quick to notice and criticize the behavior we don't like in our children. Too often our condemnation of their actions outweighs our praise. We should emulate Yitzchak's ability to see the good in a son who didn't have a lot to show for himself.

By focusing all of his attention on this noble *middah*, Yitzchak was able to elevate Esav into a paragon of *kibbud av*. The behavior we expect from our children is what they give us.

When parents make it a point to praise every success, compliment every achievement, and acknowledge every accomplishment, a child learns how to think positively about himself. The obvious question is, won't it spoil the child to be praised so often? The answer is no, not at all. It can, however, actually *spoil* a child not to be praised enough. In over twenty-five years of clinical practice, I have never once treated a patient who complained that his parents praised him too much.

(Dr. Meir Wikler, Partners with Hashem, p. 30)

Yitzchak said, "Come near and kiss me, my son." He approached and kissed him, and he smelled the scent of his garments and blessed him.

(Bereishis 27:26–27)

Yitzchak was 123 years old, and Yaakov was 63 years old. Yet they showed affection and respect by kissing each other. Children need affection from their parents to feel loved. Kissing their parents also helps children demonstrate respect.

If Yitzchak was asking his children to kiss him when they were sixty-three, surely he was doing so when his sons were small. Since children tend to be more affectionate with their mothers than their fathers, especially when they're older, this verse underscores the need for fathers to show affection for their children as well, even when they're older. Of course, this should be done with respect for the child's physical boundaries. Sefardic Jews have a custom that children kiss their parents' hands. This might be an alternative for older children who may not appreciate mushy kisses on the cheek.

The voice is Yaakov's voice.

(Bereishis 27:22)

Although Yitzchak was blind and Yaakov was dressed to feel and smell like Esav, and although it would probably not be too difficult for Yaakov to disguise his voice to sound like his twin brother, Yitzchak was still able to recognize the voice of his younger son. What he recognized was Yaakov's essence. Although Yitzchak was blinded — figuratively and literally — to Esav's true nature, he was able to discern the unique quality of his son Yaakov.

Knowing our children is paramount to raising them properly. "You have to know your child — what stimulates him or her. Become acquainted with his or her strengths and weaknesses" (*Make Me, Don't Break Me*, p. 33, quoting the Vilna Gaon on *Mishlei* and others). Truly and deeply knowing your child, and loving your child for what he is, is the key to bestowing on your child the appropriate blessings.

Vayeitzei

Bilhah conceived and bore Yaakov a son. Then Rachel said, "God has judged me; He has also heard my voice and has given me a son."

(Bereishis 30:5–6)

Although their sons are among the twelve tribes, Bilhah and Zilpah aren't considered matriarchs of Israel. We see in the verse that Rachel claims Bilhah's son as her own.

But God hasn't given Rachel a son. Why does she claim it as hers? Although Bilhah gave birth to the child, Bilhah's son was raised in Rachel's tent under Rachel's influence and guidance. It was Rachel who oversaw the spiritual education of the child.

If a person teaches a child Torah, it is considered as if he has given birth to them (*Sanhedrin* 19b). Parenting a child doesn't necessarily mean only that one has given birth to him. It means loving him, providing for his needs, and imbuing him with values. When parents adopt a child, they are regarded as the child's parents even though the child still has halachic responsibilities to his natural parents. The child's successes are considered to be in his adopted parents' merit.

Bityah becomes the paradigm of ideal parenthood. Biology plays less a role than selfless concern. She had "borne"

Moshe because she had raised him. The true parent is one who equips the child to live his life as God would have him live it.

(Of Parents and Penguins, p. 29, citing Megillah 13a)

Yaakov said to his brothers, "Gather stones!"

(Bereishis 31:46)

Rav Shlomo Wolbe asks, who was Yaakov talking to? He had only one brother, and Esav wasn't there at the time, so whom was Yaakov calling "his brothers"? The Midrash (*Bereishis Rabbah* 74:13) explains that he was referring to his sons.

Rashi explains this *midrash* [saying] that as soon as Yaakov's children were capable of helping their father, Yaakov called them his brothers. Once they could assist their father in his time of need, they became Yaakov's partners.

From Yaakov we learn to turn our child into our partner so as to give him the impression that in some specific way he is our equal, our assistant and partner. By doing so, we lighten the child's burden. He does his work happily, since his work makes him feel important. A child who learns to assist his parents achieves a new status in the home. He feels like his parents' "brother." He feels he has a purpose, and therefore he develops a more positive self-image. Also, when individuals learn to accept responsibility as children, there is a much better chance they will grow up to be responsible adults.

(Planting and Building, pp. 38–39).

Lavan awoke early in the morning; he kissed his sons and daughters and blessed them.

(Bereishis 32:1)

This is the third time in the parashah that Lavan's grandchildren are called his sons. Parenting doesn't stop with one's children. Grandchildren need their grandparents' love and attention. It is to Lavan's credit that he loved his grandchildren as his own children.

Before parting from his daughters and grandchildren, Lavan kisses them and blesses them. It's interesting that this occurs early in the morning. It is at this time that parents take leave of their own children for the day. The feelings generated by how we part from our children in the morning stay with them all day. The intensity of their desire to return home is commensurate with how they leave it in the morning. Are they rushed out of the house with "Get going, you're late," or are they held and kissed and wished a good day?

Lavan blessed and kissed his daughters and grandchildren because he knew he was never going to see them again. Although it may be a bit dramatic to part from our children every morning as if for the last time, the truth is that we never know when is the last time we do anything. If we were to live each day as if it were our last, we certainly wouldn't start it off yelling at our children and rushing them out of the house.

Let us start our children's day off right — with a hug, a kiss, and a blessing.

Vayishlach

So he divided the children among Leah, Rachel, and the two maidservants. He put the maidservants and their children first, Leah and her children next, and Rachel and Yosef last.

(Bereishis 33:1–2)

This division seems odd. Wouldn't it make sense to put the children together last in order to protect them best? And doesn't this division indicate a favoritism that would cause jealousy and friction? Wouldn't it have made more sense to put the mother with the greatest number of children in the back?

According to the Radak, Yaakov kept the children with their own mothers because maternal love would motivate the mothers to do everything in their power to protect their children. Also, being with their mothers would help the children feel more secure. And there is the added sense of security that comes with knowing their mothers were safe. Additionally, they would feel that they were protecting their mothers, giving them a sense of power. The Radak adds that this would make the mothers' prayers stronger as well.

Yaakov placed himself in front so that he would bear the

brunt of Esav's attack should there be one, giving his family a chance to escape.

Although the division of the mothers and children could be interpreted as a show of favoritism, it could also be interpreted as an indication of strength. Rachel was Yaakov's favorite, but she was also the younger of the wives. If there is strength in numbers, Yosef, being an only son, should therefore be last. The wives' status was superior to that of the maidservants, and therefore they received greater consideration. Yaakov not only demonstrated clever military strategy; he showed familial diplomacy as well.

We learn from this that in times of crisis families should stick together and take care of each other. Although there are stories, particularly from the time of the Holocaust, where parents saved their children by giving them over to non-Jews, there are as many stories of mothers and daughters, fathers and sons, who survived because they stayed together, giving each other encouragement and hope.

The strength that families provide one another is immeasurable. We cannot overestimate the power of a family's love for one another. In a time of crisis, there is no greater source of support. We also cannot overstress the importance of a mother's prayers for her children. These are sometimes the greatest weapons against the threat of outside dangers, be they physical or spiritual.

Vayeishev

Yisrael loved Yosef more than all his sons since he was a child of his old age, and he made him a fine woolen tunic.

(Bereishis 37:3)

Rabbah the son of Mechasya said in the name of Rabbi Chama the son of Gurya who said in the name of Rav: A person should never [treat] one son differently from his other children. As a result of the two *selas*' weight of silk that Yaakov Avinu added to Yosef above [that he received by] his brothers [for the cloak of many colors], his brothers became jealous of him. This led to our forefathers descending to Egypt [where they were enslaved].

(Shabbos 10b; Megillah 16b)

The disaster with Yaakov's children did not occur during the years that their father devoted more time in transmitting his knowledge to Yosef. The brothers recognized that Yosef was a prodigy and deserved having more teaching time invested in him. But when Yaakov made Yosef the multicolored silk coat, that is when the brothers were provoked. Yosef did not need to be rewarded for his greater innate talents. As far as their efforts were concerned, they were all equal, and it was the unwarranted demonstration of favoritism which led to their envy of him and the tragic aftermath.

(Positive Parenting, pp. 191–92)

To be fair, parents must give each child equal consideration, but not necessarily equal treatment. Treating all children alike is ignoring the dictum to "treat the child according to his way."

(Partners with Hashem, p. 113)

There are two places where the ten brothers acted as one: in the previous parashah, when they rescued Dinah from Shechem, and in this parashah, when they threw Yosef into the pit and then sold him to a passing caravan. (Although Reuven did not actually take part in the sale, he was part of the oath of secrecy not to reveal the truth.) One act was an act of strength for the purpose of sibling loyalty, and the other was an act of conspiracy, the archetype of sibling rivalry. Yaakov is blamed for having created this rivalry by demonstrating favoritism to Rachel's son. On the other hand, it is this favoritism that stood Yosef in good stead when he needed the strength to spiritually survive in Egypt.

The Alter of Kelm says the following: Yosef HaTzaddik said to Yaakov Avinu, "You don't have to worry about me. I was your favorite son. You gave me the colored coat. I know how much you loved me. It is because of this that I'm not going off the *derech*. I could be anywhere in the world, and you don't have to worry about me." People get the strength to resist from other people. That warm feeling, that reminder of all the *chizuk*, all the love and positive attention that Yaakov gave Yosef, that's what prevented him from doing *aveiros* (heard from Rabbi Yaakov Shapiro).

Yaakov loved Yosef more than all the other brothers, so he

singled out Yosef to study with him what he had learned in the yeshivah of Shem and Ever (*Rashi*, quoting Onkelos). Yaakov made Yosef a special tunic to symbolize his elevation to firstborn status after Reuven was discredited for tampering with Yaakov's bed (*Kli Yakar*). It was this favoritism that caused the enmity of Yosef's brothers and his exile and slavery in Egypt. But this is also what gave him the strength to endure those trials.

Furthermore, when someone is treated like they are better than everyone else, they begin to see themselves as such and develop qualities either of arrogance or of leadership. Yosef was used to being treated as someone special, so it was no surprise that this feeling was reflected to others and that everywhere he went he was shown special favor. It is no wonder that he was put in charge of Potifar's house and then of the prisoners when he was sent to prison. And it was this special quality that Pharaoh recognized when he made Yosef the royal vizier.

There is another lesson to be learned from this parashah. However you treat your children, whatever expectations you have of them, that is what they will become. If you anticipate great things from your children and treat them as if they are special, that is what they will grow up to be. If you treat your children like failures, that is what they will become.

Bas Shua, Yehudah's wife, named their second son Onan. One connotation of this name, according to the Ramban, is related to complaining and sorrow. From birth, Yehudah's son was marked for grief and failure. From birth, Yosef was used to seeing himself as special. For eight years, he was the only child of Rachel, Yaakov's most beloved wife. It is no wonder that he grew up destined for greatness. Psychological studies have proven again and again that people live up to the expectations of others for better or worse.

A new teacher in an urban neighborhood was given the worst class in the school. These were the children who'd been failing the system for years, the children that other teachers avoided. But the new teacher plunged right in, and by the end of the year the virtually illiterate class was earning A's and B's and were well behaved. The principal demanded to know how the new teacher had succeeded when everyone else had failed. The teacher said, "What do you mean? I took one look at the list of their IQ's which you gave me and kept telling them that with minds like theirs, they should have no problem learning. And, of course, they didn't." The principal turned pale. "That was a list of their locker numbers," he said.

(Our Family, Our Strength, pp. 64–65)

While parents should certainly not put undue stress on their children to achieve, nor pamper and coddle them unduly, they should encourage them and believe that they have great potential as well as intrinsic value. Yosef achieved greatness not only among his own people but as the second most powerful man in the world of his time.

Yaakov mourned Yosef's loss for twenty-two years and could not be consoled (*Rashi*, based on *Megillah* 17a). Rashi explains that the reason Yaakov could not be comforted is that he somehow sensed that Yosef was not really dead and therefore could not get past the grief.

Proof that Yaakov sensed Yosef was still alive can be found in *parashas Vayigash*: "Now I can die, after my having seen your face, because you are still alive" (*Bereishis* 46:30). Yaakov speaks of being able to die twice in the parashah, and God mentions it once. If he is ready to die now that he's seen Yosef alive, it means that he had entertained some hope of this possibility, and that is what had kept him alive. With that kind of devotion and love, it is no wonder that Yosef was able to achieve such greatness.

There is no limit to the power of a parent's love for his child. Parents need to make each child feel as if the child has the greatness of Yosef HaTzaddik within him and love each child as if he were an only child even if he shows no greater promise than Yehudah's son Onan. Because often what can turn an Onan into a Yosef HaTzaddik is the great strength inherent in the belief and love of a devoted parent.

Mikeitz

Yaakov said to his sons, "Why do you make your-selves conspicuous?"

(Bereishis 42:1)

Yaakov's plea to his children to keep a low profile repeats it-self several times in the Torah. The Talmud says (Ta'anis 10b) that it is dangerous to show the have-nots that you have. The brothers were told by Yaakov to go to Egypt so as not to appear as if they had enough to eat, and they should not enter by the same gate so as not to incite envy that one man was blessed with ten such sons.

Not showering everything on our children is difficult. We want them to have the best toys, the nicest clothes, the most ex-citing trips, the most fun birthday parties. But aside from encour aging children to value materialism, being ostentatious invites jealousy, which invites the evil eye.

This is relative, of course. If someone lives in an affluent neighborhood and invites only children from affluent homes to his son's birthday party, there's no problem. But usually that's not the case. If someone buys their child bigger and more expen-sive toys than those of the other children in the neighborhood, this invites jealousy, hurt feelings, and bitterness.

This isn't to say we shouldn't buy nice things for our children. We should just keep the sensitivities of others in mind, as well as the fact that the most expensive and elaborate things are not necessarily the most entertaining or educational.

We also need to be careful not to boast about our children. It's impossible not to rave about our kids to some extent. Every mother knows that her child is the cutest, smartest future *gadol hador* ever to be born, *bli ayin hara*. We rave, we *kvell*, we tell stories. Grandparents, spouses, and close friends who love the child are a rapt audience, but such stories can also arouse jealousy and competitiveness when told to others. And where our children are concerned, we don't want to arouse such feelings.

It's interesting that Yaakov gives the above warning after he saw what happened to Yosef, with all his praise and extra attention. We need to shower our children with love and attention, but we don't need to do it in front of the whole world.

Vayigash

He has made me father to Pharaoh.

(Bereishis 45:8)

Rav Shimon Schwab says the following in the name of Rav Michael Forschlage, who was a *talmid* of the Avnei Nezer: Rashi says that a parent is supposed to be a friend to his child. Yosef HaTzaddik said to his brothers, "*Vayesimeini l'av l'Pharaoh* — Pharaoh made me an *av* over him." Rashi asks, what does *av* mean? A friend. This is where we learn that a father is supposed to be a friend to his child.

This does not mean that the father is supposed to be on the same level as the child. Rav Forschlage says that if you want to know the meaning of any word, you look at the first time it comes up in the Torah. The first time the concept of a friend comes up in the Torah is the relationship of Chirah and Yehudah. A friend is someone to whom you can tell anything even if you committed a sin. A father is supposed to have the type of relationship with his child where his child feels he can tell his father anything, even if the child did something wrong.

A child is supposed to respect his parents and even hold them in awe, but not to the extent that when he does something wrong and needs someone to talk to, he's frightened to approach them. His parents should be the first people he goes to (heard from Rabbi Yaakov Shapiro).

Parents have to impart to their children the feeling that they are there for them when their children have a problem, no matter what that problem is, whether it's a problem at school, with friends, or with negative outside influences that can have serious ramifications.

Vayechi

In this parashah, we see wonderful examples of "like father, like son." Yaakov asks Yosef to bury him in Me'aras HaMachpeilah:

Please do not bury me in Egypt.

(Bereishis 47:29)

At the end of the parashah Yosef makes the same request:

When God will indeed remember you, then you must bring my bones up out of here.

(Bereishis 50:25)

Last requests reflect a person's priorities. Both Yaakov and Yosef's last request was to be buried in Israel. They both knew that their descendants would want to visit their graves, and they wanted to make sure that their graves were in the Holy Land. Where one is born is not under his control, but he can say where he wants to be buried. And this says a lot about him.

Our last requests to our children, whether at our bedside or, as is more common nowadays, in wills, should be a reflection of the values we want to leave to them as a legacy, not just our monetary possessions. Where we want to be buried, how much money we leave to charity, whether or not we put aside a trust fund for our grandchildren's religious education, a letter telling our children that we love them — these are all things that indicate our priorities.

Then Yisrael prostrated himself toward the head of the bed.

(Bereishis 47:31)

According to Rashi, although it is improper for a father to bow down to his son, Yaakov was really bowing down to royalty since Yosef was a reigning viceroy. We learn from this that we have to treat our children with the respect due them as human beings and, when they grow up, with the respect accorded to adults of their stature.

Many of our children grow up to be rabbis, doctors, professors, judges, dignitaries, and government officials. While other people address them as "sir," "Doctor," and "Your Honor," their parents may still address them as "Shloimke." It is important, especially in public, that parents acknowledge the official status of their children and certainly the fact that they are grown up. No matter what their stature, there are those who will look up to them as older and wiser (their children, for example), and we have to maintain that truth in their eyes.

> ...if you do not insist on seeing in the young man or woman nothing more than a mere boy and girl, if you do not forget that as they grow older they must be treated differently, and you must become friends to them in order that they may become friends to you. Then, when you have firmly linked their hearts to yours in this way, you may confidently allow them to leave you and wander abroad. Over mountains and val-

leys, over land and sea, they carry your picture at once smiling and stern in their hearts, and in the hour of temptation it will with warming mien appear to them as Yaakov's picture did to Yosef and will become their guardian angel to keep them worthy of you and save you from sinking.

(Horeb, translated by Dayan Grunfeld [New York: Soncino Press, 1981], p. 414, quoted in Make Me, Don't Break Me, p. 35)

By you shall Yisrael bless saying, "May God make you like Efraim and like Menasheh."

(Bereishis 48:20)

Every week we bless our children, quoting this verse. Blessing our children is a privilege that we have every week. This blessing reminds us that we are blessed with children. We must not for one moment take this blessing for granted, and we must utter these words with the deepest awareness of the gratitude we owe Hashem. Accompanying the blessing with a hug and kiss is also the general custom.

Efraim and Menasheh are role models for our children. Yosef's children remained righteous even though they were surrounded by a pagan culture. Today we are surrounded by a pagan culture, by the false gods of materialism and pleasure seeking. We need role models to help us combat the materialism of the Western world and the misguided spiritual influences of the Eastern world.

Making sure your children have live role models to emulate, being such a role model for your child, and making sure you read them stories of noble and self-sacrificing people from our tradition is the recipe for bringing up children who are not only worthy of blessing but who are a blessing to their parents.

He blessed each according to his appropriate blessing.

(*Bereishis 49:28*)

Yaakov goes on to bless the rest of his sons. In these blessings he points out the strengths and weaknesses of each of his sons and how they are to use these to serve God. It is imperative for us as parents to be aware of our children's strengths and weaknesses and to reflect them back to our children so that they can perfect and take pride in the former and work on improving the latter. We must instill in each child the knowledge that he has been given special gifts by God that he is to use in the service of God.

There is no sadder situation than a child who is forced to abandon his own strengths in favor of pursuing a career deemed worthy by his parents only to fail or be miserable in its pursuit. Yaakov's gift was that he understood who each of his children was, and he blessed them in accordance with each one's personality. Each of our children's gifts, be they beauty, intelligence, charm, business acumen, musical talent, appreciation of nature, or generosity, is special and meritorious. King Shlomo said, "Teach the child according to his way." This includes appreciating each child's special talents and gifts, helping him develop along the path suited to him, and praising and blessing the results.

Giving a child piano lessons when he likes to draw or making a child sit in extra Torah classes when he'd rather go collecting mushrooms in the woods is torture to the child. A child must be given the blessings meant for him. Blessings also include opportunities. Giving a child the opportunities to develop himself according to his inclinations will make him a source of blessing both to his parents on earth and to his Father in Heaven.

The blessing Yaakov gives each of his children is a blessing in disguise. It appears that Yaakov is cursing his children or condemning them by comparing them to animals or pointing out their flaws. Rav Zev Leff points out that the greatest blessing you can give a person is the blessing of self-knowledge. Yaakov did just that by pointing out his children's weaknesses as well as their strengths. Yaakov pointed out their strengths, as he did with Yosef: "A charming son is Yosef.... His bow was firmly emplaced, and his arms were gilded" (*Bereishis* 49:22–24). And he pointed out their weaknesses, as he did with Reuven: "Water-like impetuosity — you cannot be foremost" (ibid., 4). That is our job as parents.

The blessings conclude with "All these are the tribes of Israel" (ibid., 28). None of the sons had more or less status in the family. Each one was a tribe — because of his strengths and in spite of his weaknesses.

Whatever strengths or weaknesses we perceive in our own children, we have to let them know that they are all equal in the eyes of their parents, that they are equally important to the family.

SHEMOS

לכו בנים שמעו לי, יראת ה׳ אלמדכם.

Go, O sons, heed me;
the fear of Hashem I will teach you.

(Tehillim 34:12)

Shemos

With Yaakov, each man and his household came.

(Shemos 1:1)

Rav Shamshon Raphael Hirsch explains that although each son had his own family, he remained united with Yaakov, like a branch growing from a stem. The concept of a family tree is not only a quaint metaphor. Children are like apples who don't fall far from the tree, but it's important for them to feel part of the tree in the first place. It's important for children to spend as much time as possible with their grandparents, aunts, uncles, and other extended family. This gives them a sense of their roots and their continuity and hopefully teaches them to respect their elders.

Although nowadays the extended family is usually extended geographically as well, it's worth the effort to keep in close contact even if this is sometimes difficult and expensive. Today communication has never been easier, with the phone, e-mail, pictures, video. Family togetherness is important for a healthy sense of self and sets an example you'll want your children to follow when they leave home to start their own families.

But as much as they would afflict it, so it would increase and so it would spread out.

(Shemos 1:12)

The nation here is referred to in the singular because every Jewish child born increased the strength of the nation as a whole. Even though the Jewish people were afflicted by Pharaoh and even threatened with punishment and death, they continued to bring Jewish children into the world. Recognizing children for the national and personal treasure they are and having the attitude that each child is a blessing worth sacrificing for was one of the basic tenets of the Jewish nation even in its infancy.

She could not hide him any longer, so she took a wicker basket and smeared it with clay and pitch; she placed the child into it and placed it among the reeds at the bank of the river.

(Shemos 2:3)

The episode of Moshe being hidden among the bulrushes teaches us many lessons in parenting. One is that it teaches us to look for creative solutions. Often we don't use enough creativity in finding solutions.

Once, when my son was a couple of months old, there was a performance I wanted to attend. I was nursing full-time, and the distance I needed to travel would have entailed too long an absence. I called the theater and asked if they could find me a place where I could leave my baby with a friend who had offered to babysit. The management of the theater agreed. Not only did I not have to choose between seeing the performance and nursing my son, but we got VIP treatment, and my son was personally serenaded by members of the orchestra, who found they had a captive and delighted audience.

His sister stationed herself at a distance to know what would be done with him.

(Shemos 2:4)

Miriam earned great merit for her devotion to her brother. That was one of the reasons she was so severely punished for her evil talk against him later. It was because she was so close to him, like a second mother.

Perhaps that was what contributed to Moshe's greatness. At three months old he had three very devoted mothers — Yocheved, Miriam, and Bityah.

Children should be involved in the help and caring of their siblings. As Rav Eliyahu Dessler explains, the more you give to someone, the more you love them (*Strive for Truth*, vol. 1, "Lovingkindness"). It follows, then, that the more involved children are in their siblings' care, the more love they're going to feel for them.

> It is often the mother's attitude toward life that provides the older siblings with lessons in loving by giving. To teach her family to be aware of others and to care for one another is the utmost any mother can hope, pray, and strive for, from the moment she brings her baby home. This is the beginning of her child's education to Torah and mitzvot.
>
> (*Straight from the Heart*, p. 104)

She saw the basket among the reeds, and she sent her maidservant, and she took it.

(*Shemos 2:5*)

It isn't clear if the last *she* in the verse refers to Bityah or her maidservant. According to Rashi, quoting the Sages, the Hebrew word *amasah* means not "her maidservant" but "her arm." Although she was far from the basket, Bityah stretched out her arm as far as she could. God extended it to the point that she could reach the basket. Thus "she took it" refers to Bityah.

Child-rearing often seems difficult, but God endows parents with superhuman strength when they need it most, especially mothers. All they have to do is make the initial effort. We all know how difficult it is to cope on only a few hours of sleep a day, yet mothers with small children do it for weeks and sometimes months at a time. Parents are capable of superhuman feats because they have superhuman love for their children.

Another possibility is that Bityah sent away her maidservant and took the basket. The common adage "If you want something done, better do it yourself" is very applicable to child-rearing. No one is more capable of meeting the needs of a child than a mother. Sending her maidservant away and reaching for it herself, then instructing Miriam to get the child's natural mother, shows Bityah's good sense in recognizing the hierarchy of those best suited to meeting the needs of a child. The birth mother is the natural choice. If, for some reason, the mother cannot be there, then it should be someone who is as devoted as a mother, and if not, only then find hired help.

She took pity on him and said, "This is one of the Hebrew boys."

(Shemos 2:6)

Compassion is the key to being a good parent. Bityah felt compassion for Moshe and knew she could save this child's life. Miriam saw this immediately, and so without hesitation she offered to find a wet nurse.

We get irritated with our children when they're fussy or frustrated or unhappy. What we need is a dose of compassion. We can show compassion by understanding the child from his point of view. Bityah saw Moshe's plight — a child whose life was threatened and who was separated because of this from his mother. We need to recognize the daily plights of our children, major and minor, and show them compassion even if we're not feeling queenly that day.

Pharaoh's daughter said to her, "Take this boy and nurse him for me, and I will give your pay."

(Shemos 2:9)

Usually one hires a babysitter to look after the child, ironically at three months (usually the length of paid maternity leave). She entrusts her child to another woman, whom she pays to feed and take care of him. Here Pharaoh's daughter gives three-month-old Moshe back to his mother for her to nurse.

A child recognizes his mother and responds to her best. It's the mother's job to bring up her children, and it is the mother who is supposed to nurse her children, and the Talmud recommends nursing for a period of at least two years (*Shulchan Aruch, Even HaEizer* 82:1).

When a child is properly cared for and nurtured, he will thrive. According to the Gemara (*Berachos* 54b), Moshe grew to be ten *amos* tall (that's twenty feet!).

A mother also provides spiritual nurturing as no one else can.

I once heard of a gentile nanny who took care of a child and put him to bed every evening, since the mother worked at that hour. One day the mother stayed home and put the child to bed herself. "Wait, Mom," said the child, "I cannot go to bed until I say my prayers." Then he kneeled near his bed and made the sign of the cross on his chest.

The astonished mother asked, "Where on earth did you learn to do that?"

"From the nanny" was the innocent reply.

(Beloved Children, p. 176)

The boy grew up, and she brought him to the daughter of Pharaoh, and he was a son to her.

(Shemos 2:10)

In the very next verse it says, "Moshe grew up and went out to his brethren and observed their burdens." Since Moshe was treated with such compassion, first by his mother, then his sister, then his foster mother, he was able to show compassion. We see this also in Moshe when he asked innocently, "Why would you strike your fellow?" (*Shemos* 2:14). Whatever trait you want to instill in your child, you must display to him.

According to Rashi, Moshe went out purposely to see the slaves and empathize with them. He then suggested to Pharaoh that they be given one day of rest (*Shemos Rabbah*). The effect a child has on the world when he grows up will be influenced by what kind of upbringing he had. Therefore, when we raise our children, we are not only affecting their future but the future of all the people they will come in contact with throughout their lives.

Moshe's trait of feeling compassion and acting on it also led to his finding a wife — when he saved her and her father's flocks at the well.

They came to Reuel, their father. He said, "How could you come so quickly today?"

(Shemos 2:18)

The interchange between Reuel (Yisro) and his daughter seems fairly benign. He asked why they had come early, and they told him.

Now these weren't little girls; these were young women. Yet their father noticed and took an interest in their daily routine. Reuel was a minister, a priest and a leader; he was a busy man. Yet he had time to notice the variation in routine of his daughters.

If you sent your teenager to the supermarket to buy some mineral water, would you notice if it took her fifteen minutes more or less than it usually does? Would you think to ask why? Reuel did, and as a result he merited to become the father-in-law of the greatest prophet of Israel.

> A parent who always asks his child where he is going and when he intends to be back is giving the child the message that he cares and that the child must account for his actions. When your child comes home, ask him to tell you about what he did. Do this in a casual way, so that he will not feel that he is being interrogated. The child will soon learn that he has to account for his time and his actions and that he cannot do whatever he likes.
>
> (*Beloved Children, p. 268*)

Each woman shall request from her neighbor and from the one who lives in her house silver vessels, golden vessels, and garments; and you shall put them on your sons and daughters, and you shall empty out Egypt.

(*Shemos 3:22*)

I can understand asking for the possessions, but why put them on the sons and daughters?

Whatever we do has an effect on our children. We leave them not only a physical legacy but a spiritual, psychological, and emotional one as well. Our children observe our behavior and integrate it into their own personalities, even against their will.

The riches from Egypt were not only spoils to be taken and passed on to the next generation when the hoped for freedom would come. The Israelites were commanded to show their children where the riches had come from and how they went about getting them. In this way, their children would not forget that their parents were once slaves and God had freed them, endowing them with the wealth of their oppressors.

The message here is that when we want children to understand a concept, they must not only be told but they must be shown as well.

So Tzipporah took a sharp stone and cut off the foreskin of her son and touched it to his feet.

(Shemos 4:25)

Moshe set off for Egypt without circumcising his son. Because of this, an angel met him on the journey and threatened to kill him. Tzipporah understood why her husband was in danger. She immediately took matters into her own hands and circumcised her son.

There are certain mitzvos that are incumbent on men and others that are incumbent on women when it comes to child-rearing. When a father is unavailable for whatever reason, it is often possible for the mother to perform the mitzvos that the man is obligated to do and vice versa. The same way a father wouldn't let his child go hungry if the child's mother weren't around to nurse him, a woman shouldn't let a child starve spiritually because of her husband's failure or inability to perform a certain mitzvah.

If a father isn't around to teach a child Torah or circumcise him or buy him tzitzis or build him a sukkah, a mother can do so. According to the Gur Aryeh, Tzipporah realized that the immediate threat of danger to Moshe's life was a way of prompting her to circumcise the baby immediately. She was the first (and to my knowledge last) female *mohel* in history.

So said Hashem, "My firstborn son is Israel...."

(Shemos 4:22)

God calls Israel His firstborn. Pharaoh therefore is acting in the capacity of a foster parent of sorts. But he is a strict disciplinarian. When Moshe comes to seek the nation's freedom, Pharaoh tells them "You are lazy! Now go to work," and he refuses to give them straw (see *Shemos* 5:18).

In reaction to Israel's desire for freedom, Pharaoh gives them more restrictions. This makes them more rebellious and more anxious for freedom. So it is with our own children. If they refuse to do what they're told and toe the line, they are often given even more restrictions and are expected to follow even stricter demands. But this usually doesn't work. Too many restrictions lead to rebelliousness.

Often, children who perceive their lives as slavery break out of bondage and escape, never to return. We must learn from Pharaoh's bad example not to make our children feel like they are in bondage. When our children indicate that their burden is too heavy, we need to look for ways to lighten it.

Va'eira

So Moshe spoke accordingly to the children of Israel; but they did not heed Moshe, because of shortness of breath and hard work.

(Shemos 6:9)

To continue the analogy from the previous parashah, once a child becomes bitter and rebellious, he won't listen to anyone, even those who mean his good and are trying to help him. A few verses later, the tribes are listed according to their families. The key to having well-adjusted children is by bringing them up in families. The family must be a cohesive unit. That isn't to say that single parents won't raise well-adjusted children. I hope I have. The key to a healthy family unit is not the number of people in it but the fact that they are a unit. The Jewish people are a nation "according to their families" (*Shemos* 6:17).

Hashem shall distinguish between the livestock of Israel and the livestock of Egypt, and not a thing that belongs to the children of Israel will die.

(Shemos 9:4)

God gave the children of Israel their livestock and referred to it as belonging to them. Some parents tend to be cavalier about the possessions of their children, taking them away as a punishment, forcing them to share or give away their precious possessions ("after all, it's only a doll/puzzle/dress"), using their stuff without asking permission. Having their own possessions gives children a sense of identity, and, when they're able to acquire possessions, a sense of responsibility and, hopefully, appreciation. We can't hope for our children to develop these traits if they don't feel their possessions are really theirs.

Pharaoh kept promising to give the children of Israel their freedom and then time and again reneged on his promise. We must be true to our word and not be "Egyptian" givers. When we give, it should be forever.

Hashem carried out this word the next day.

(Shemos 9:6)

There are four aspects to this verse that teach us our responsibility to keep our word to our children (or anyone for that matter):

"Hashem" – Hashem made the promise, and He was the One who carried it out.

"Carried out" – He did what He promised.

"This word" – what Hashem did was the exact thing He said He was going to do.

"The next day – He did it at the appointed time, without delay.

Promises must be kept and fulfilled in their entirety to the last detail.

Bo

...so that you may relate in the ears of your son and your son's son.

(Shemos 10:2)

The primary responsibility of educating and instructing children falls on the parents. How do they do this? Through talking to them — by speaking "in their ears." Not to their backs or by voice mail, but by sitting down and talking to them face to face so that their message penetrates. This is how to pass on values, family history, and moral lessons.

Moshe said, "With our youngsters and with our elders we shall go; with our sons and with our daughters, with our flock, and with our cattle we shall go, because it is a festival of Hashem for us."

(Shemos 10:9)

Many mitzvos are best done as a family, whether you're serving Hashem at the Shabbos table, celebrating a wedding, or going on vacation on Chol HaMo'ed. Of course, it isn't always convenient, practical, or even economical to always celebrate with the entire family. Sometimes parents need to spend time alone together, and occasionally kids like to spend Shabbos with friends. But if the family always splits up on Shabbos and for *simchah*s and for vacation, when are families going to be together?

A family should be together as much as possible. It should be the norm, not the exception. Care should be taken and efforts should be made, especially at festive occasions, to celebrate them as a family. The seder night should not be the only time when the entire family is together.

He said to them, "So be Hashem with you as I will send you forth with your children! Look — the evil intent is opposite your faces."

(Shemos 10:10)

As the Ramban explains, Onkelos interprets this verse as saying that Pharaoh told Moshe that Moshe's "evil intent" not to return was clear; otherwise, why take the children along? Pharaoh could not understand why the nation would take the children along to celebrate its festival.

It is only after the plague of darkness that Pharaoh agrees to send the children. This is symbolic, since light is a metaphor for Torah, and children are compared to a Torah scroll. Pharaoh felt the absence of light in the same way the nation would feel the absence of the children.

But for all the children of Israel there was light in their dwellings. Pharaoh summoned Moshe and said, "Go, serve Hashem.... Even your children may go with you."

(Shemos 10:24)

The nation is always referred to as the "children of Israel" and, by extension, the children of God. When it comes to serving God, we are all children — children of the Almighty.

And it shall be when your children say to you, "What is this service to you?" you shall say, "It is a Pesach feast offering to Hashem...."

(Shemos 12:23)

Children learn by asking questions. Often parents get irritated by the incessant stream of questions children ask. They often perceive of them as annoying, time-consuming, or insubordinate. Children ask questions because they need to know the answers. And God Himself tells us to answer our children's questions. We need to give legitimacy to their questions by showing them that what they care about is important to us, or they'll stop asking. Worse, they may decide to ask the wrong person.

Children are our future. When did Pharaoh finally release the slaves? When the future of Egypt was threatened. Egypt suffered the loss of its water, its physical safety, its livestock, the health of its citizens, its crops, and its sanity. Each time, Egypt recovered and went on, but when the children began to die, they couldn't take anymore. With the children gone, there would be nothing left — no hope, no future. Our children are our number one priority because they are our future.

This is why the mitzvah of telling our children is superimposed on the plague of the firstborn. This alludes to the fact that if we don't educate our children properly, we might, God forbid, lose them to the dangers of the world.

Sanctify to Me every firstborn.

(Shemos 13:1)

The first time we do anything we do it with tremendous enthusiasm. The same is true of raising children. There's the old joke of how the firstborn child has an entire album of baby pictures, while the second child only has a couple. Whether or not this is true, how we raise the first child sets the tone for how we raise our subsequent children. Though we may make mistakes with our firstborn that we won't repeat with subsequent progeny, we do put our greatest efforts into our first children.

God tells us to sanctify the firstborn. If we raise our first child in an atmosphere of *kedushah*, with a love for mitzvos, and inculcate him with a feeling of self-esteem, then doing the same with the other children will be easier and come more naturally.

The Jewish people are considered God's firstborn. Every child is therefore one of a nation of firstborns.

Beshalach

Pharaoh will say of the children of Israel.

(Shemos 14:3)

The verse uses the words "*livnei Yisrael*," which mean "*to* the children of Israel," even though he was really speaking *about* the nation. This teaches us that when we talk *about* someone it is as if we are talking *to* them, because usually what is said about people reaches them eventually.

Parents often talk about their children, whether it's to complain or to *kvell* or just to share their experiences. But what effect do our words have on them? Do our children get the impression that we love them and are proud of them? Do they feel they're a burden or a disappointment? We must always choose our words carefully when speaking not only *to* our children but also *about* them.

Needless to say, we must strictly observe the rules of *shemiras halashon* when talking about our children.

And the people revered God, and they had faith in God and in Moshe His servant.

(Shemos 14:26)

As parents, we are God's representatives on earth. We expect our children to listen to us, to love us, and to revere us. It is our responsibility to be worthy of their respect and love. Do we act like God's representatives, by protecting them, being there for them, coming through for them in a crisis, answering them when they cry out to us, and keeping our promises, teaching them how to serve God? While it's our children's obligation to honor us, it is our obligation not to make it difficult for them to do.

Then Moshe and the children of Israel chose to sing this song to Hashem.

(Shemos 15:1)

Miriam the prophetess, the sister of Aharon, took her drum in her hand, and all the women went forth after her with drums and dances.

(Shemos 15:20)

Moshe led the nation in song, as Miriam led the women in dance. When we want a group of people to behave a certain way, we have to set an example. If we want our children to act a certain way, we have to model that behavior.

Moshe led the nation in a song of praise and thanks to Hashem. How often do we tell our children to say thank you, to be appreciative, especially to us? There is no better lesson than showing by example. Moshe Rabbeinu didn't tell the nation, "Now pray. Now give thanks." He himself sang a song of praise to Hashem. A good leader, a good parent, a good teacher, sets a good example. We have to become the kind of people we want our children to be, and then they will emulate us.

This is my God, and I will build Him a Sanctuary; the
God of my father, and I will exalt Him.

(Shemos 15:2)

What will our children worship and consider their top priority? Money, family, social status? Whatever parents worship,
that is what their children worship, provided that there's a good
relationship between parents and children. Children have been
known to rebel and worship exactly the opposite of what parents
worship, but more likely children will emulate their parents' values.

Moshe said unto Aharon, "Say to the entire assembly
of the children of Israel, 'Approach the presence of
Hashem, for He has heard your complaints'...."
Hashem spoke to Moshe, saying, "I have heard the
complaints of the children of Israel."

(Shemos 16:9–12)

Everyone, especially children, needs to feel heard. Parents
need to really listen to their children. If a child has a complaint,
the parent should hear it and then determine if it is justifiable. If
it is a valid complaint, the parent should try to remedy it if possible. Bear in mind that a child views all his complaints as valid.

One day I went to visit a friend and brought her two daughters stickers of ornate flowers. The packages were the same, but
the individual stickers weren't. The girls were upset because
each one wanted some of the stickers the other one had, not all,
but some. I stood and watched as their mother mixed and
matched the stickers, moving them from one package to the
other until the girls were satisfied with the combination each
had acquired. The mother understood the need for each girl to

have her preferences honored and accorded the situation the same gravity due to partitioning up land to world powers.

Even more than solving a child's problems, a parent must listen to him. A person who feels heard feels understood, and a person who feels understood feels valued. A person who feels valued feels good about himself and contributes positively to society.

Yisro

"I, your father-in-law Yisro, have come to you, with
your wife and her two sons with her." Moshe went
out to meet his father-in-law, and he prostrated himself and kissed him, and each inquired about the
other's well-being.

(Shemos 18:6–7)

Yisro is a good example of how to be a good parent to your
children after they marry and a good in-law. Yisro took back his
daughter and her children to live with him when it was dangerous for her to stay with Moshe. At the first opportunity he took
her and his grandchildren to be with Moshe again.

The relationship between Yisro and Moshe, two of the most
important men of their time, is a great lesson to us in familial re-
lations. When Moshe came to Midian, Yisro the high priest wel-
comed Moshe into his home. When Moshe became the leader of
the Jewish people and was busy guiding an entire nation of two
million people and had to be prepared to greet the Shechinah at
any moment, he took the time to sit and talk to his father-in-law
and update him on recent events.

We are all so terribly busy and overburdened. Although in

our hearts and minds our families are our first priority, often they take a back seat to many less important things. We can learn from the meeting between Yisro and Moshe that when family visit, they come first, no matter what other pressures and commitments we may have.

The father-in-law of Moshe said to Him, "The thing that you do is not good. You will surely become worn out."

(Shemos 18:17–18)

The "thing" that Moshe was doing was judging every case the nation brought to him on his own. Many times our children ask us to judge between them and their siblings or friends. This increases exponentially with every child and every friend. It can be wearying. But this is not our job. A parent can't judge between his children because he is not impartial and he is unaware of all the facts. Therefore he can't be fair, and neither will his judgment be fair.

It is a parent's job to offer empathy, love, and understanding. If a parent delegates the authority of solving disputes to the children themselves, there will be far less disputes and far more peace. And, like Moshe, the parent will have to deal only with the really big "cases," as it is written, "Then you will be able to endure, and this entire people as well shall arrive at its destination in peace" (*Shemos* 18:23).

Honor your father and your mother.

(Shemos 20:12)

The Torah states some very clear rules about how a parent is to be honored by his child. It includes, the Gemara tells us, doing *chesed* for the parent, for example, bringing him a drink; standing up for him when he enters a room; and not interrupting him when he is talking. How do we teach our kids to do this? By honoring our own parents.

As we said before, children learn by example. The simplest way to teach our children to honor us is to honor our own parents. If our parents are no longer living, we can honor their memories by giving *tzedakah* for their *neshamos*, lighting *yahrtzeit* candles, sponsoring a *kiddush* or *shiur* in their memory, or starting a *gemach* in their name. By honoring our own parents, we are acting as role models for this mitzvah. We provide an opportunity for our children to merit long life.

Mishpatim

Distance yourself from a false word; do not execute the innocent or the righteous.

(Shemos 23:7)

While many wouldn't think of themselves as liars, some people at times are less than truthful. Not keeping promises and making less than truthful excuses are both examples of instances where parents may lie to their children. Not only are they undermining their children's trust; they're setting a bad example to emulate.

It's very important to keep a promise even if you preface it with *"bli neder."* Disappointment is difficult for anyone to swallow, but even more so for a child. If you promise a child a special treat or reward, make sure you give it to him, or tell him beforehand that the expected reward will have to be delayed should he earn it.

Another common example is parents using children to make excuses for them. "Tell Hindy I can't come to the phone because I'm not here." Not only are you teaching a child to lie by example, but you're actually instructing him to do it. Once a behavior begins to be ingrained in a child, it's very difficult to reverse it.

Casting blame on children is often condemning the innocent. Children are an easy mark for our anger and suspicion. And we figure, "Well, even if he didn't do what we're blaming him for, he must have done something else, so he deserves a punishment anyway." We tend to disbelieve a child if he says, "I didn't do it," yet believe another child if he blames the first child. This doesn't make sense, and it isn't fair.

Children have an absolute sense of justice. If they're falsely accused of something, they may very well say, "As long as she thinks I'm guilty, I might as well do something wrong."

We must give our children the benefit of the doubt because they don't always have the tools — either developmental or emotional — to accurately explain what happened.

Terumah

You shall make two cherubim of gold....

(Shemos 25:18)

The *Mechiltah* comments that all the items in the Mishkan could, if it was difficult to get gold, be made of other metals. The exception was the cherubim. Why? The cherubim had to be made of pure gold because they represented the children, who are innocent and pure. And their place was on top of the *Aron* (where the tablets were kept) — to symbolize that we have to teach our children Torah.

From this we learn that in Torah education we aren't exempted with copper coins, only gold. Our children's education has to be dear to us, and we have to be willing to invest in it.

There are many people, especially abroad, for whom Jewish education costs a fortune, who claim they can't afford it. Jewish education is very expensive, and if you have a number of children, it can be prohibitive. Yet many of these same parents come up with the money for music lessons, camp, trips, and the latest fad for their children. They eschew Jewish education but find the money for everything else because they don't want the children to feel deprived.

Yet, depriving a child of a Jewish education is depriving him of the most important thing. It's like feeding a child candy but saying you can't afford bread. Yes, children need extracurricular activities, and camp and trips but only after they have the basics. The same way you first feed your child bread and chicken and then give him sweets, a child should first be given a Torah education and then, if there's time and money, the extras. The same way a parent always finds ways to feed his children physically, he should use the same amount of creative energy to provide spiritual nourishment for his children. If the parent chooses the other things over a Torah education, he's setting a precedent for the child, who may later choose the extras over a Torah life.

You shall make the Tabernacle of ten curtains — twisted linen with turquoise, purple, and scarlet wool — with a woven design of cherubim shall you make them.

(Shemos 26:1)

The entire parashah of *Terumah* focuses on what one could call interior decorating. What's more, this decorating applies to the most spiritual thing in the physical world, the Tabernacle.

Every physical object has a spiritual energy. Beautifying the physical enhances its spiritual manifestation. We see this regarding the concept of *hiddur mitzvah* — buying the most beautiful *esrog*, using fine china on Shabbos. If God requested physical adornment for His Sanctuary, then surely we need a pleasing environment to inspire us emotionally and spiritually.

Some might consider things like decorating superficial luxuries. But if God saw the need for curtains of a specific color and fabric, surely it isn't frivolous to provide our children with an environment that is pleasing to them and meets their aesthetic needs.

The visual and tactile needs of children change every few years (every few months for younger children). It is important to provide them with an environment that encourages their development at every stage within the parameters of the family budget. The same way we try to ensure that our children's environment is safe, we should also ensure that it is stimulating and pleasing to them. (It is also a good idea to encourage children to contribute their input in designing their environment.)

They shall make a Sanctuary for Me so that I may dwell among them.

(Shemos 25:8)

Children can also contribute to the décor of the home. Framing children's paintings and artwork or even putting their pictures on the fridge makes them feel like they have made a contribution as big as that which *bnei Yisrael* gave to the building of the Mishkan. Every Jewish home is supposed to be a mini sanctuary. All of Israel was meant to bring forth a contribution "from every man whose heart motivates him" (*Shemos* 25:2). Similarly, when children present their creations to their parents, they are motivated by devotion and a desire to please.

Tetzaveh

You shall take the vestments and dress Aharon with the tunic, the robe of the *eifod*, the *eifod*, and the breastplate, and you shall girdle him with the belt of the *eifod*.

(Shemos 29:5)

Tetzaveh deals at great length and in great detail with the vestments of the *kohen gadol*. Besides describing the clothing, the commentators explain what each garment symbolizes and its spiritual purpose.

Many Jewish mothers are familiar with the *kohen gadol*'s raiments, usually because it is one of the first Purim costumes young children wear. Purim provides for young children something they need for their development — the chance to dress up, to pretend, and to try on new roles. As the parashah states, clothes play a major part in taking on a role. Clothes also play a very important part in children's development. Whether it's using costumes for make-believe, dressing up like Mommy or Daddy in role-playing games, expressing their independence by choosing their own style, or adopting certain dress codes that show membership within a certain group, clothes play a symbolic as well as practical role in children's lives.

It's important, therefore, to be aware of what clothes represent to children at the different stages of their lives. Young children need the opportunity to try on different roles as they grow up and mature. Keep a trunk or bag of old clothes so they can "try on" the role of king, queen, kohen gadol, or even bandit to allow them to explore different sides of themselves. Teenagers need to be allowed a certain amount of freedom with their wardrobe. Clothes are a way for them to express their individuality as long as Torah values are not compromised. And when a child grows up, he adopts the style of dress that is appropriate for the community in which he has chosen to live.

Finally, it's important to remember that it's the human being under the clothes that's important, the neshamah under the hat or kippah of whatever size, shape, and color, the Yiddishe kop under the hat, scarf, or wig.

He and his vestments, and his sons and his sons' vestments with him, shall become holy.

(Shemos 29:21)

It isn't what you wear so much as what you do when you wear it that gives you an aura of holiness.

Ki Sissa

The wealthy shall not increase, and the destitute shall not decrease from half a *shekel*.

(Shemos 30:15)

This parashah speaks of the contribution of the half-*shekel* coin everyone between the ages of twenty and sixty gives. Today we have a custom to give a *tzedakah* contribution before Purim in commemoration of this mitzvah.

In a family, all members are building a mini sanctuary. To this end everyone must contribute. The bulk of the work should not fall to the parents. Children should be expected to give their share each in his own way. Not only does being a contributing member build self-esteem and help develop important life skills in the child, with our busy schedules it is absolutely necessary.

Very young children can contribute by watering plants, feeding fish, bringing things from another room, or sorting laundry. Older children, aside from taking care of their own clothes and possessions, can take turns clearing and setting the table, doing dishes and laundry, and taking out the garbage. Teenagers can go grocery shopping and cook.

It's important for kids to feel needed and successful, and seeing a job well done does exactly that. Children can also be expected to earn their own pocket money. Younger children can do special jobs at home, and older children can babysit or clean for others. "When giving an allowance or paying children for chores, it's important to pay children their 'wages' on time" (Chafetz Chaim, *Ahavas Chesed* 9:5).

The status of Israel is elevated by its contributions to charitable causes, and this is why they were counted by having the entire nation join in contributing to a sacred cause. This concept is emphasized by the literal meaning of the commandment (*Shemos* 30:12) "When you elevate the heads of the children of Israel..." (*Bava Basra* 10b; *Pesikta Zutresa*). This implies that the function of these contributions was not only to facilitate a census and to provide for the Tabernacle, but also to raise the spiritual level of those who contributed.

The equal participation of all the people symbolizes that all Jews must share in achieving the national goals, by giving up his selfish, personal interests for the sake of the nation. One who does so gains infinite benefit, because the mission of Israel is dependent on the unity of the whole (Rav Shamshon Raphael Hirsch).

As with the nation, so with the family, the subsection of the whole. And along with all this, it is important to give family members roles that neither overtax them by being beyond their capabilities, nor insult them by being too easy. A certain amount of choice, negotiating, and trading may also be necessary.

Most importantly, don't take what your children do for granted. Make sure to praise them for their efforts and say "thank you." Allow for a messy training period, but have faith that in time they'll learn the ropes and that eventually each family member's contribution will be invaluable.

Remember how you reacted when your children learned to walk. How do all parents react when their child takes their first step?

After the child takes the first step, they become excited. They hug and kiss the child. They telephone their friends and relatives. The child feels the excitement and appreciates the recognition. The child is probably thinking, *You think I did well this time? You just wait and see what I'll do next time!*

(Make Me, Don't Break Me, p. 45)

The people saw that Moshe had delayed in descending the mountain.... "We do not know what became of him."

(Shemos 32:1)

According to Rashi, the delay perceived by the nation was a mistake in mathematics. Whatever the reason, when Moshe was "late," the people panicked. If a nation that had just witnessed divine revelation couldn't handle their leader being a few hours late, *kal vachomer* our own children should not be left without supervision for any unreasonable time. This isn't to say we shouldn't trust them or grant them independence, but they should know we are never far away.

We should also be very careful to return at the appointed time if we go away for a few hours or a few days and clarify that our children understand when that is. This is important for keeping babysitters as well as retaining credibility with our children. Nowadays, people left to their own means don't worship golden calves, but children who are left too long unsupervised may engage in equally dangerous and self-damaging behavior. Also, parents lose their aura of authority if they absent themselves too long from their children. They have to be around in order for their influence to be felt.

He [Moshe] said, "Not a sound shouting strength nor

a sound shouting weakness; a sound of distress do I hear!"

(Shemos 32:18)

It is a well-known fact that mothers can distinguish between the different cries of their infants. They can determine just by listening whether their baby needs to be fed, changed, or just held. Sometimes we lose the ability to distinguish between the different distress signals of our children. There's interference from other sources demanding our attention, and when our children express a need for something, we often don't hear the real request behind the words.

When Moshe came down from Sinai, Yehoshua told him there was the sound of battle in the camp. Yehoshua was still an apprentice, so he wasn't able to distinguish between the sounds the people were making. But Moshe, who had assumed leadership over a year earlier, was already a veteran. He knew what had transpired because God had just told him what was going in the camp, but he chose to call it a cry of distress.

Ramban, citing a *midrash*, comments that Moshe's answer was an implied rebuke to Yehoshua, as if to say that the future leader of Israel must be able to detect the people's mood by the way they sound.

Parents must know their children. To know them, they have to (a) spend time with them and (b) listen carefully to what they say. A request for a new toy may in fact be a request that the parent spend time with his child. A complaint against a sibling may be a plea for more attention or affection. We have to hear the subtext behind the words. Children aren't always capable of expressing themselves or are often embarrassed to do so. Not every ten-year-old boy would feel comfortable asking his mother for a hug, so he might complain about his sister instead.

Touch is the universal language of love. Yet it is a need that some modern parents dismiss as unessential.

(Raising Children to Care, p. 89)

Although many of our cherished hypotheses in psychology have been seriously challenged through the years and have fallen by the way, the need for love and affection as a foundation for healthy growth remains relatively unchallenged.

(Dr. Agnes Hatfield, Affectional Deprivation and Child Adjustment, p. 54, quoted in To Kindle a Soul, p. 115)

Sometimes requests or complaints are straightforward, and we must listen and acknowledge the need behind them even if we can't always fulfill the requests. As adults, our needs aren't always logical or practical, but we give ourselves permission to have them, and quite often we give into them. Children don't usually have that power. They are dependent on us to provide them their requirements and desires. This puts us in a position of power. We mustn't abuse that power and discern what it is our children are truly asking for. "The greatest service of God lies in the purification of motive" (*Strive for Truth*, vol. 1, p. 99).

Moshe said to Aharon, "What did this people do to you that you brought a grievous sin upon it?"

(Shemos 32:21)

This is a lovely example of giving someone an opportunity to defend himself by giving the benefit of the doubt. Although Moshe's question is meant as a rebuke, he still gives Aharon an out. He assumes that the people must have done something to Aharon to make him behave in such a manner, and he gives Aharon the opportunity to defend himself. He doesn't shout accusations and condemnations at him.

Rabbi Abraham Twerski, a noted psychiatrist and author, relates that when he was a child and did something that didn't find favor with his father, his father would say to him, "*Es past nisht* — That is not becoming of you." This served the double purpose of letting his son know that the behavior was wrong and boosting his self-esteem by indicating that such behavior was beneath the dignity of a person such as himself. By rebuking Aharon in this way, Moshe gave him the same message. He expected more of the *kohen gadol*.

When parents are angry, they often yell at and demean their children. Not only does this sometimes prove to be unfair, since there may be a good reason for the child to have acted that way, but it makes the child feel like a bad person. It destroys his self-esteem. Many educators and psychologists point out that self-esteem is the most important tool for a human being to have a happy and productive life. It is incumbent upon us to build self-esteem in our children and to help them understand that we expect them to act positively because they are positive and valuable people.

> Every parent should feel that his child is destined for greatness. We can inspire the development of that greatness in our children by giving them the gift of self-esteem.
>
> (*Beloved Children, p. 310*)

And You shall forgive our iniquity and error and make us Your heritage.

(*Shemos 34:8*)

Over and over again the people sin, and over and over again God forgives them. Sometimes He punishes them; sometimes He looks the other way. God, in His abundant mercy, always forgives them. God forgave the people for continually sinning against Him and repeatedly declared that no matter how much His children sin against Him, Israel will still remain the chosen people and will ultimately be blessed.

Sometimes children commit a thoughtless act; they behave badly, whether against others, against their parents, or against God. No one should be more righteous than God Himself. Whatever our children do, they should know that they are loved unconditionally and will be forgiven. Most of our children are not guilty of horrible, heinous acts. Parents should always leave room for a child to repent. Even if a child goes off the *derech* or rebels in an intolerable way, the children have to feel that they have somewhere to return to, when they want to return.

If God could forgive His children's sins, we should be able to forgive ours.

Do not cook a kid in its mother's milk.

(Shemos 34:26)

Divorce is not a pleasant thing. It can be awful for children, especially if they are at a vulnerable age. What's even worse than the divorce itself is when children are forced to choose sides, when one parent tries to turn the child against the other parent. This is like cooking a child in its mother's milk. A child who sees one of its parents as the enemy cannot help but see himself as the enemy because both parents are part of the child. Turning a child against a parent is like turning a child against himself. Inevitably he feels guilty, which only aggravates the situation.

Parents don't have to pretend they have nothing but loving feelings toward the other parent. That's obviously not so. But the acrimony should remain between them. The same way the great love and intimacy that existed before was kept private, the great resentment, hurt, and anger should be kept private. A parent shouldn't speak negatively about the other parent, no matter how much he feels provoked, in front of the children. If you can't say anything nice, don't say anything at all. If trouble is brewing, get the children out of earshot.

Vayakhel

You shall not kindle fire in any of your dwellings on the Sabbath day.

(Shemos 35:3)

In *The Ultimate Win/Win* (published by Targum Press), Rabbi Moshe Goldberger says, "Children should not perceive of Shabbos as the time when parents have more time to yell at them." Anger is compared to fire (*Tikunei Zohar* 55). Both leave devastation in their wake. While no time is a good time for anger, Shabbos, which is called a "taste of the Next World," should be reminiscent of Heaven, not Gehinnom. We want our children to love being with us on Shabbos and to love Shabbos as well, which is the source of all blessing (*Etz Yosef* on *Zohar*; *Iyun Tefillah, Shabbos* 118a). We need to ensure that the one time a week the whole family is together, no fires, physical or emotional, burn or smolder.

Pekudei

The stones were according to the names of the sons of Israel, twelve according to their names, like the engraving of a signet ring, each according to his name, for the twelve tribes.

(Shemos 39:14)

Three times the Hebrew word for "name" is mentioned in this verse. A person's name is very dear to him. It's exclusively his. It is the dearest word to him in any language. Children like to hear their names.

We have to be careful what we call our children. If we give a child a nickname, we need to make sure it is a term of endearment and not of derision.

We need to remember our children's names. How often do parents who are blessed with many children go through a list of their children's names before they get to the one they are addressing? That can't be good for helping children develop their individuality.

Each tribe had its own stone, a symbol of each one's individuality. Each stone signifies a different type of physical and spiritual energy that matches the name of the tribe.

The following story, recounted in *To Kindle a Soul* (pp. 32–33), illustrates poignantly and convincingly how what we call our child determines his nature and self-conception:

The Gordon family (not their real name) decided to take their five children, all under the age of ten, on a trip to Netanya, a beach town about ninety minutes from their Jerusalem home. Mrs. Gordon took each child to the bathroom before the family departed from home and once again at Jerusalem's central bus station. Mr. Gordon purchased tickets for the express bus to Netanya.

About an hour into the bus ride, their five-year-old son, Yaakov — who since birth had been called by the affectionate nickname Kadosh (Hebrew for "holy one") — turned to Mr. Gordon and announced, "Abba, I have to go to the bathroom."

"Didn't you go before we left home," Mr. Gordon asked in surprise, "and again at the bus station?"

"I didn't have to go then," the child answered innocently. "I have to go now!"

Yaakov's father responded calmly, explaining that the express bus couldn't stop, but that they would arrive in Netanya soon and there would be restrooms there. Yaakov was content for about fifteen minutes, but then he complained again, this time with a bit of panic in his voice. "Abba, I have to go. I really have to go!" Mr. Gordon, now lacking the confidence that his little Kadosh was going to last, approached the driver, but was unable to impress upon him the urgency of the situation. The driver retorted that "this is the express bus, and the express bus doesn't stop."

By the time the bus arrived in Netanya, Yaakov had assumed the posture of a pretzel, and his agonized moans frightened his brothers, sisters, and parents. With the older children blocking traffic, Yaakov and his parents quickly descended from the bus, Yaakov alternately skipping and limping toward the sign that read "Restrooms." Upon reaching the restrooms, the Gordons were dismayed to see wooden boards blocking the entrance and a sign: UNDER CONSTRUCTION. Yaakov's face filled with panic.

"Don't worry," one of the older children said, running toward the nearby promenade, "we'll find you a restroom!" The older children tore off down the street, looking for a store with facilities, and Yaakov, now held up by his parents, tenderly danced along behind. Yaakov's brothers and sisters ducked quickly in and out of stores. No luck. They disappeared around a corner.

Then suddenly they reappeared, sprinting toward Yaakov with glee and shouting, "We found a bathroom! We found a bathroom!" Grabbing their brother by the arms, they started walking him quickly toward the end of the block.

"Where's the bathroom?" Mrs. Gordon called to the children.

"In a bar," one of them called back.

"What's a bar?" Yaakov asked between quick breaths.

"It's a place where people get drunk and listen to loud music," another child answered him.

The five-year-old Kadosh stopped in his tracks.

"What's wrong?" Yaakov's older brother erupted.

"I can't go into a bar," the little boy explained.

"Why not?" Mr. Gordon demanded.

Yaakov looked up at Mr. Gordon ingenuously and answered, "Because I'm Kadosh."

The spiritual image that the Gordons had cultivated in their son about himself was stronger than the physical needs of his still immature body. Imagine what kind of power our appellations exert over our children's psyche. What's in a name, indeed!

Why did the *kohen gadol* have to wear the names of all the tribes on his breastplate? Couldn't he remember them? The parental equivalent would be carrying around pictures of one's children. It's not because we don't remember what they look like; it's because they are so dear to us that we want to look at them whenever possible and feel they're with us constantly.

> Like everything that Hashem commanded Moshe, so did the children of Israel perform all the labor. Moshe saw the entire work, and, behold! They had done it as Hashem had commanded, so had they done! And Moshe blessed them.
>
> (*Shemos* 39:42–43)

The children of Israel had erected the Tabernacle according to God's instructions, and Moshe blessed them. Our children, though they may follow our instructions, may not always achieve the desired result. Does that mean they are not deserving of appreciation for their efforts or accomplishments? How often do we find fault with our children's efforts instead of expressing appreciation for what they have done? This is destructive. It sets up a no-win situation where the child feels that nothing he does is right and sees himself as doomed to failure. When our children complete a task, we should praise them. And if they did it because we have asked it of them, we should bless them.

VAYIKRA

הנה נחלת ה׳ בנים, שכר פרי הבטן.

Behold! The heritage of Hashem is children;
a reward is the fruit of the womb.

(Tehillim 127:3)

Vayikra

Speak to the children of Israel and say to them.

(Vayikra 1:2)

The commentators note the apparent redundancy. Rav Shamshon Raphael Hirsch comments that *daber*, "speak," denotes brief, concise expression, referring to the Written Torah. *Amirah*, "saying," was God's explanation of the Torah.

We speak to our children in different ways. We speak, we say, we tell, we remind, we nag…. Sometimes we tell them concisely what we want them to do in the form of a directive, and sometimes we explain things to them at length.

There are appropriate times for each form of communication. If a small child is about to touch something dangerous, we shout a clear "No!" to stop him. However, if an older child is contemplating doing something we feel is destructive, we are more likely to explain to him why we don't feel this is a good idea. On the other hand, when teaching a small child *derech eretz*, we will go into detail and explain at length why walking around undressed is inappropriate, whereas if an older child wants to wear something immodest, a simple "Not that!" is sufficient to remind him of the earlier message.

It's important to know which situation requires which kind

of discourse. Aside from age, factors such as the nature of the individual child, the situation, and time constraints all influence the choice. What's important is that we do not brush off a child who begins to argue when an explanation is necessary, nor go into a lengthy diatribe when a concise request or demand is required.

Speech is just one of the tools at our disposal for *chinuch*. We need to know how to make the best use of it, taking advantage of all the nuances of communication at our disposal.

> If one's offering is from the flock, from the sheep, or from the goats for an elevation offering, he shall offer an unblemished male.
>
> (*Vayikra 1:10*)

The Hebrew word for "unblemished" is *tamim*, which connotes purity and innocence. If we want our children to live elevated lives, they need to have a certain amount of purity and innocence.

Maintaining the balance between sophistication and innocence in our children is delicate, if not precarious. We don't want their souls to be sullied with information that can confuse them and take away their youthful perspective. On the other hand, we don't want them to be so innocent that they unknowingly put themselves in danger by trusting too much or being ignorant of what can happen to them in certain situations. This is to a large extent a personal as well as cultural issue, depending on where and how you live.

However, it is important to remember that it isn't appropriate to expose children too early to things to which they need have no knowledge. When necessary, a parent should give a child the information in the simplest way without extraneous details. In that way the child will feel comfortable confiding in his parents and approaching them if there is something he wants to talk about.

Differing viewpoints exist on speaking openly to a young person on the subject of adolescence. The son of the Chafetz Chaim tells us that his father talked to him when he was fifteen years old and began by saying, "After this I will no longer speak to you on this subject." He then explained to his son the whole subject of cautiousness in holiness. Some feel that it is better to leave the subject without discussion, assuming that the child will learn on his own through the various laws explained in Torah books. It is difficult to decide in this matter, but in general a young person should not be left completely alone or undirected, for without guidance he may become confused and distressed. At all times, we must be sensitive and aware of his problems, giving him an open door to discuss them with us and receive our support and understanding.

(The Eternal Jewish Home, pp. 87–88)

Tzav

The *kohen* from among his sons who is anointed in
his place shall perform.

(Vayikra 6:15)

The *kehunah* passes from father to son. Unlike the other
tribes, the *kohanim* have a permanent job waiting for them from
the day they are born. The tradition passes from father to son for
all time. Although the *kehunah* is a biological legacy, there are
still tools of the trade that a *kohen* teaches his son.

The Talmud teaches that a father is required to teach his son
Torah, a trade, and, according to one opinion, how to swim
(*Kiddushin* 29a). It is incumbent upon a father to make sure that
his child has the means to make a living in order to provide for
himself and his family.

While many children don't want to follow in their fathers'
footsteps, a good place to start teaching a profession is with
one's own. While parents should certainly make it clear that a
child should follow his own path, they can at least introduce him
to their professions to give him his first exposure to work. While
the actual vocation may not be what the child has in mind, a
child can learn a lot about work from watching his parents.

Many children are brought to work for the day during school

vacations, and many get their first summer job at their parents' place of work. Besides introducing children to the work ethic, this also helps the child understand his parents better and leads to parent-child bonding. For parents with teenagers, this can be a generational bridge that provides for common ground. By watching a parent at work, a child can learn about initiative, follow-through, responsibility, integrity, and teamwork.

This is the teaching of the guilt offering; it is most holy.

(Vayikra 7:1)

What's so holy about a guilt offering? The fact that a person is able to admit his mistake, to admit he's wrong. It is a sad state of affairs if a person can't admit he's erred and say he is sorry. Whether out of insecurity or arrogance (two sides of the same coin), pride or fear, many people find it difficult to admit they're wrong. This causes friction between employers and employees, friends, spouses, and most particularly children. Why particularly children? Because one is passing on the legacy of not taking responsibility and rectifying one's mistakes.

The act of admitting you're wrong teaches many vital lessons. First, it shows it's okay to be human and relieves the pressure of some children who feel they have to live up to their parents' real or imagined high standards. Second, it teaches children to admit when they've made a mistake. Third, it provides the opportunity to show what can be done to rectify a mistake. Fourth, it makes the person who was wronged feel better. He sees that others are sensitive to his pain, which also teaches empathy. Fifth, a child feels valued when a parent asks him for forgiveness.

The real measure of parents and teachers is not whether they make mistakes, but whether they make valiant efforts to avoid repeating them.

(To Kindle a Soul, p. 24)

According to the halachah, one is supposed to ask a person he has wronged or hurt for forgiveness (Mishnah, *Yoma* 8:9; Rambam, *Mishnah Torah, Hilchos Teshuvah* 2:9).

Rabbi Wasserman says that parents definitely should apologize to their child in such situations and that it will improve their relationship with him.

(More Effective Jewish Parenting, p. 48)

What also makes this offering so holy is that admitting you're wrong and asking to be forgiven is difficult. It takes a lot of strength of character to do so. In fact, the greater the misdeed, the greater the damage and pain caused, and the closer the person who was affected by the mistake, the harder it is to admit, the harder it is to ask forgiveness, and the harder it is to make amends.

God wants us to learn from our mistakes and to grow by fixing them. If you haven't done so in the past with your children, a good place to start would be asking for their forgiveness for having never apologized before. If David HaMelech could admit his mistake when confronted by Shmuel HaNavi (*Shmuel* II 11:13), we certainly can.

As important as asking for forgiveness is learning to give it. In this we emulate Hashem by being merciful and gracious. We must set an example for our children in asking and granting forgiveness, and thereby we will set up a cycle of regret and forgiveness, love, and kindness.

Hashem spoke to Moshe saying, "Take Aharon and his sons with him...."

(Vayikra 8:1)

According to Rashi, *kach*, "take," in the verse means "win him over with words." Aharon felt unworthy of the task and had to be persuaded. It's interesting, paradoxical, and difficult to believe that the leader of Israel had to convince Aharon to assume the priesthood. One would think he would be thrilled with the honor or, at the least, Moshe could order him to do it as an emissary of God.

We learn from here that it is better to use gentle words of persuasion than order someone to do something even if it's something important and for his own good. Many times parents pull rank to get children to do things when there are better ways of getting children to cooperate, whether it's to volunteer for a project, join a group, or enter a contest. The child may be unwilling, either because he doesn't feel ready, good enough, or have the drive to do it. Often, if a parent demands rather than gently coaching and lovingly prodding, it doesn't yield good results. If the child doesn't succeed or derive anything positive from the undertaking, he'll resent the parent. If in the end he does succeed and enjoy himself, he'll still feel bad, because he was forced into it and can't take pleasure in his own accomplishment since it wasn't his idea in the first place.

In the end, Aharon did assume the priesthood, but Moshe led him every step of the way, washing him, dressing him, and equipping him for the job.

Shemini

Hashem spoke to Aharon saying, "Do not drink intoxicating wine, you and your sons with you, when you come to the Tent of Meeting, that you not die — this is an eternal decree for your generations."

(Vayikra 10:8–9)

Rabbi Yishmael is of the opinion that this law, told to Aharon immediately following the death of two of his sons by divine fire, implies that their death must have been punishment for entering the Sanctuary having drunk more than the permitted amount of wine. Although Jews use wine to sanctify Shabbos and holidays and for other ritual purposes, with the exception of Purim a Jew is not supposed to drink. He is supposed to serve God with a full heart and a clear head.

If Nadav and Avihu, on their high level, were able to go over their limit in the desert, we have to be a hundredfold more cautious with our children today when alcohol is massively available and so easy to get.

In *parashas Noach*, we saw the dangers of overindulgence. In the same way that we teach our very young children that they must take a sip of Kiddush wine, they must learn to stop there. Wine, alcohol, liqueur, like everything else, must be used to serve God. If it's used for anything else, tragedy can result.

If great men like Nadav and Avihu can have their senses blurred by alcohol so that they present God with an alien fire, how much more must we safeguard our children so that they, too, do not become sacrifices, God forbid.

Tazria

She shall bring a sheep within its first year for an elevation offering and a young dove or a turtledove for a sin offering....

(Vayikra 12:6)

These were the sacrifices offered by a woman after giving birth. The sin offering was to atone for having thoughts not to conceive again while enduring the pain of childbirth (*Niddah* 31b).

When things get difficult, in childbirth or child-rearing, a woman might say she doesn't want to have any more children. Nevertheless, children are God's blessing to us, and bringing them into the world and raising them as devoted Jews is part of our job — the most important part. It is unappreciative of us to be upset at God for our role as parents. Obviously I am not speaking about women who have postpartum depression or who find child-rearing extremely difficult because of a physical or emotional condition that makes motherhood less joyful. These women often have rabbinic dispensation to limit the number of children they have. Nor am I talking about women whose children, due to some condition they suffer, pose a burden which adds to the usual trial of parenting. I'm talking about the average woman with the average child who resents her job as a mother at times when the child isn't throwing oatmeal in her hair or crying with colic for the seventh time that evening.

I have been asked by a good friend to mention the fact that many overwhelmed mothers sometimes feel like advertising their children for sale in the classifieds but don't because they can't think of any selling points. Parents, especially mothers, are often exhausted and in their sleep-deprived state are less than loving and tolerant. This is normal, as long as it is short-term. However, if this feeling persists, or if a parent becomes abusive, the parent needs either physical assistance or emotional counseling from a supportive counselor or rabbi.

In order to be good parents, we have to love being parents. If we don't love it, we have to focus on the perks — the warm hugs and soft kisses, the smell of a newly washed infant, the giggles of a toddler, the glowing report cards, the look that's only for you, and just the fact that there's another human being in the world with your freckles who calls you "Mom."

There are thousands of women going through unspeakable physical pain and emotional anguish to become parents. The same way we bless our food many times a day even when we're not particularly hungry or the food isn't especially tasty, we as mothers have to bless God for our children, even when we're tired, even when they're going through the terrible twos or adolescence, even when they remind us of our worst character traits. They are ours, and we are blessed to have them. We should try to make maximum use of our potential as parents even if it involves a sacrifice.

"This is the child I have prayed for" (*Shmuel* I 1:27). It is this child that we have for which we should show our gratitude.

Metzora

I will place a *tzara'as* affliction upon a house in the land of your possession.

(Vayikra 14:34)

God placed the affliction of *tzara'as* in three places: the walls of the sinner's home, his clothes, and his skin. The sinner had three chances to redeem himself, and if he didn't, the affliction would get closer and closer to him.

When there's a problem in the home, in the family, we tend to minimize it. We say it's no big deal and it will work itself out. If the problem grows, it becomes more apparent; it extends beyond the home, and we are literally washing our dirty linen in public. If we continue to ignore the problem, it takes over our lives so that anyone can see it just by looking at us.

When a major problem crops up at home, it should be dealt with immediately. Its importance should not be trivialized. Every issue that affects the family has to be addressed; otherwise, it will spread and affect everyone in the family and become apparent to everyone around them. By then the family may need outside help. We have to learn to read the writing on the wall so that we can contain our problems before they spread.

Acharei Mos

Any man shall not approach his close relative to un-
cover nakedness....

(*Vayikra* 18:6)

This parashah speaks of forbidden unions between various
family members. These unions take into account, among other
things, blended families — parents who have remarried due to
death or divorce of a spouse and the various permutations that
could result from the union: half-sisters and -brothers, stepsis-
ters and stepbrothers and stepparents. In such situations, care
must be taken to respect the privacy and dignity of each family
member. While affection and closeness should be encouraged in
blended families, physical and emotional boundaries must be
respected. Attention must be paid when children complain, especially at the beginning, that their needs are not being attended
to and their limits aren't being respected.

A certain amount of adjustment is necessary in any new living arrangement. No complaint should be trivialized, especially
when siblings or parents of the opposite sex are involved.

Because of the dramatic and sudden nature of the changes in
everyone's lives, all rules and limits need to be openly and

frequently discussed, stated clearly and concretely, and im-
posed on a trial or temporary basis only. The rules also need
to be reevaluated and closely monitored for how they affect
all concerned.

(Partners with Hashem, p. 289)

Although this relates to all aspects of the new living arrange-
ments, special sensitivity must be shown to the feelings of the
children regarding the more personal and private aspects of
their lives. This includes knocking before entering a room, even
one's own if it's shared; perhaps having a separate bathroom for
each gender; respecting rules for modesty of dress around the
house; not reading other people's messages or mail; avoiding
eavesdropping; and respecting every individual's need for his or
her own physical space.

Kedoshim

You shall not place a stumbling block before the blind.

(Vayikra 19:14)

According to the Rambam, in his *Sefer HaMitzvos*, this commandment forbids someone from causing anyone else to sin. Children are required to honor their parents. This includes various mitzvos like not calling them by name, not contradicting them, and not sitting in their seat. Parents should make it easy for their children to show them the proper respect by inspiring the child's love and trust. Some parents insult their children, embarrass them, don't listen to them, and don't show sensitivity to their needs. They undermine their children's efforts or their sense of security and self-esteem and then expect their children to show them respect. Respect and honor are like everything else — behaviors that are learned. If we want our children to show us the respect the Torah says we deserve, we have to model the behavior we desire.

> The father is forbidden to impose too heavy a yoke on his children, to be too exacting with them in matters pertaining to his honor, lest he cause them to stumble. Rather, he should

forgive them and shut his eyes, for a father has a right to forego the honor due him.

*(Shulchan Aruch, Yoreh De'ah 240:19,
cited in More Effective Jewish Parenting, p. 55)*

In *Criticizing Children* (p. 22), Avi Shulman writes that we teach our children how to treat us by our verbal and nonverbal messages:

> The story is told about a little boy who went to play with his neighbor. His mother called him in for supper several times, but he totally ignored these calls. When asked by the neighbor why he didn't respond to his mother's frequent calls, he says, "Until she calls eight times, she doesn't even have supper ready!"

If we want to inspire respect in our children, we have to be fair and consistent. We also have to display sensitivity to their feelings. "We are not only obligated to be sensitive to these feelings," writes Shulman, "but our ability to win or, *chas v'shalom*, lose the child's respect is based on this sensitivity" (*Criticizing Children*, p. 28).

You shall not commit a perversion of justice; you shall not favor the poor, and you shall not honor the great; with righteousness you shall judge your fellow.

(Vayikra 19:15)

Sometimes parents feel they have to act as judge and mediate between their children. When the children fight among themselves or even disagree with the other parent, the parent feels he or she has to jump in to judge the case.

A judge is supposed to be unbiased, and a parent is anything but objective. He may favor one child because the child is younger or always being picked on or, alternatively because he's older, brighter, or more like the parent. A parent should certainly teach the rules of fair play and point out to an older or stronger child the advantage he has over his siblings so he won't abuse it, but the parents should not actively take sides in disputes between children. Rabbi Shlomo Wolbe, in *Zeriah U'Binyan B'Chinuch* (p. 43), advises the parents to let the children work it out themselves: "The most a parent can do, when no one's life or limb is at stake, of course, is to analyze his own behavior to see if he is in any way contributing to the situation."

In *Beloved Children*, Rabbi Yisroel Pesach Feinhandler also suggests encouraging children do nice things for each other and say nice things about each other in order to build brotherly love. At the Shabbos table, each child could tell a story about something nice one of his siblings did that week. If you keep your children busy looking for good in their siblings, they'll have less time to fight.

> Instead of deciding who is right, try to pinpoint mistakes that each side has made, such as hitting a brother, acting with anger, or insulting one another. You can show each child what his mistake was without getting involved in the question of who was right and who was wrong in this particular fight. This way you will stay impartial and will not be taking sides and causing hurt feelings.
>
> (*Beloved Children*, p. 229)

You shall reprove your fellow, and do not bear a sin because of him.

(Vayikra 19:17)

It is our duty to discipline and guide our children, but we are not to act sinfully in trying to correct their errant behavior. Rashi (quoting *Sifra*) says it is wrong to embarrass someone when reproving him. Parents know better than anyone else what will embarrass their child. Not only will embarrassing a child have the opposite effect and not mend the behavior, but it will cause the child to foster resentment against the parents, which will lead him to rebel. Causing a child to rebel is the greatest stumbling block you can place in front of him.

Embarrassment also destroys self-esteem in children, which is the single most necessary ingredient for them to succeed in life and be happy, contributing members of society capable of actualizing their potential. The danger of embarrassing children cannot be overstated.

Reb Simchah Zissel of Kelm noted that the best way to reprove is in small gradual steps. Stating bluntly that someone did something wrong will only antagonize him. Reproving someone in small doses at repeated intervals is much more effective and is less likely to backfire.

You shall love your fellow as yourself.

(Vayikra 19:17)

This certainly applies to children. Put yourself in your child's place and then treat him the way you would want to be treated if you were the child. According to Rochel Frumin, marital and family counselor and co-coordinator of the Maor Einayim Creative Therapy Center in Jerusalem, if you treat your children in the way you would have liked to be treated as a child, you ease the pain of your own childhood.

> Children's feelings are real. When they cry, they are sad. Even if they seem to cry all day long, they feel sadness with each episode. Their anger is real each time, as are their fear

and their joy.... The frequency of the emotion does not diminish its intensity.

(A Delicate Balance, p. 127)

Loving someone is feeling both his joy and his pain as if it were your own, not only when you understand its cause, but even when you don't. When a child knows you share his feelings, he feels loved.

Loving our children also means wanting them to be successful. Children often have special projects and activities that are dear to them. We can help them be successful in their endeavors by encouraging them, helping them if they ask, or being resource people. When we respect our children's interests, applaud their successes, and share their disappointments, we are being the best example of how to "love your fellow."

Emor

These are the appointed festivals of God...which you shall designate in their appropriate time.

(Vayikra 23:4)

This parashah lists the festivals and the times they are celebrated. Imagine trying to celebrate the holidays at the wrong times. Imagine having a bonfire on Tu BiShevat or making hamentaschen or challos for Pesach or fasting seder night or dressing up in costume on Yom Kippur. Disaster, right? Insane! That's what happens when we try to make things happen at the wrong time.

Our children develop according to a preprogrammed timetable. We don't expect our children to walk at two months or to be speaking in complete sentences at six months. Yet in many ways we rush their development unrealistically. We expect emotional, developmental, spiritual, or physical maturity before they are ready. This only puts pressure on them, frustrates them, and lowers their self-esteem.

If we expect a six-year-old child to sit through three hours of davening without a break, not only are we setting him up to fail, but we're instilling a hatred of shul. If we expect our daughter to become a little mother at the tender age of seven and care for her younger siblings for hours at a time, we're depriving her of her childhood.

Often parents want their children to grow up too quickly. The irony is that with that kind of pressure they never do. A child has to completely and fully experience each stage of development in order to grow out of it, or he never completely finishes with it and moves on.

We want our children to succeed. We want to make sure they reach their potential. But we sabotage their progress as soon as we make unrealistic demands on them. A child will reach his potential only if he's properly nurtured, not if parents keep raising their expectations. Schools and society put enough pressure on children to succeed. When children come home from school, we must allow them to explore who they are and be who they are. We must let them grow and take shape in the appropriate time. If you don't know what behavior is age appropriate for your child, do some research. If you don't know if you're causing your child stress, ask him.

Young children characteristically like to learn and do and help. They don't need to be pushed into it. They have a lot of initiative. Let them set the pace. In many cases it's better to demand too little than too much. Look out for symptoms of stress in your child: irritability, lack of appetite or eating too much, insomnia, bedwetting, nervous twitches, rebelliousness, confusion, depression, and exhaustion. Any of these could be a sign that your child is feeling he is under too much pressure.

Our jet-set society is more concerned with training, mislabeling it "discipline." Modern mothers rush to train their babies as quickly as possible to fit into the adult world. After all, society teaches us that babies are a burden and an inconvenience to their parents, whose "precious time" could otherwise be spent far more productively. By getting them onto schedules right away, introducing solids as soon as possible, and weaning them before they are ready, we try to make them into baby-adults, causing ourselves and our children much sadness and frustration. This egocentric approach only slows down the natural process for growth and maturity.

(Straight from the Heart, p. 109)

Just as it is impossible to eradicate natural tendencies of character, it is impossible to ignore a child's developmental stages. In vain do zealous mothers toil to accustom their children to matters that by virtue of their age should not yet become issues. Even if such parents succeed, they may actually harm their child! It should be clear: Any demand that is incongruous with a child's age is liable to wound his tender heart, a wound which can in the future have a worrisome effect on his development and personality. This [effect] can find expression in the form of fears, nervousness, and lack of independence at an age that demands independence.

(Alei Shor, Ma'amar HaChinuch, p. 263,
quoted in My Child, My Disciple)

...for it is the Day of Atonement to provide you atonement before Hashem, your God.

(Vayikra 23:28)

On Yom Kippur, we get the chance to have our slates wiped clean. We are cleansed of our sins and forgiven for our transgressions — at least as far as God's concerned. Parents, on the other hand, seem to have their own method of scorekeeping. They recall every misdemeanor, mistake, and misjudgment committed by their offspring from the day they were born. And in case their children have forgotten, they remind them. But it is forbidden to remind a person of his previous sins if he has done *teshuvah* for them (*Bava Metzia* 58b).

> Although it is sometimes hard to remember the child in previous stages, it can be equally difficult to forget that earlier child. Long after a child has matured and learned his lessons, a parent may hold an image of an irresponsible, impulsive youngster requiring constant supervision and direction. The parent may refuse to forgive the child for mistakes he made long ago. Failure to forgive is, in itself, incompatible with Torah directives, for we are obligated to learn how to forgive others completely (*Bava Kama* 93a). A parent who frequently reminds a child of his past wrongdoing makes it clear that forgiveness has not been granted. Moreover, we are cautioned about reminding people of their misdeeds (*Shulchan Aruch, Choshen Mishpat* 228:4). Such reminders reinforce a child's negative self-concept.... If a parent truly desires that his child grow and change for the better, he must be willing to look for improvements and comment on them.... Most important, he must not remind the child of occasions on which his behavior was unacceptable.
>
> (*A Delicate Balance, pp.* 138–39)

Wouldn't it be wonderful if instead parents used this capacity for recollection to recall their children's successes and triumphs, record them in a book or an album, and take them out periodically to show them?

These are the appointed festivals of God that you shall proclaim as holy convocations, to offer a fire offering to God: an elevation offering and its meal offering, a feast offering and its libation, each day's requirement on its day. Aside from God's Sabbaths, and aside from your gifts, aside from all your vows, and aside from all your free-will offerings, which you will present to God.

(Vayikra 23:37–38)

The book of *Vayikra* is full of sacrifices that God commands us to offer to Him: sin offerings, peace offerings, daily offerings. These sacrifices were replaced by prayer. Why do we have to offer up so many prayers and sacrifices to God? Does He really need so much reinforcement of our devotion to Him?

We are being taught to recognize our love by expressing it. Perhaps God is also trying to teach us that when we love someone, we have to constantly show him. "He knows" is not good enough. Not for God – and not for our families.

Our children need to be shown time and time again that we love them, are devoted to them, are proud of them, enjoy them. We can do this in many ways – saying "I love you," buying them gifts even when there's no special occasion, being present at an important event (a school play, an awards ceremony, "firsts," graduation) to cheer them on, spending one-on-one quality time with them, writing them notes and leaving them in their schoolbags or on their door, calling them when they or you are away. Our children have to know that they are first and foremost in our thoughts. If God, Who can read our innermost thoughts, requires of us that we demonstrate constant devotion to Him, *kal vachomer* our children who can't read our minds and often misread them.

We must include our children in our busy lives. Rabbi Noach

Orlowek, in his book *My Child, My Disciple*, even suggests taking children out of school in order to spend time with them.

> Clearly, raising children successfully is not a part-time job. It requires a total commitment. Our children must feel they are our first priority. They must feel loved. They must feel that we're more concerned with their well-being than our social life, finances, or appearance.
>
> Though the years may seem endless, children are not children for very long. When we get bogged down with making money or advancing our careers, we miss the one-time opportunities in their childhood. On the other hand, the relationship will endure throughout our lives if we put effort into their early years.

(Our Family, Our Strength, p. 54)

Command the children of Israel that they take to you clear olive oil, pressed for lighting, to kindle a continual lamp.

(Vayikra 24:2)

Light, especially candlelight, has always played an important role in the lives of the Jewish people. Light has spiritual as well as practical qualities. Having a continual light burning in the Mishkan and Beis HaMikdash was symbolic of the fact that God is always on call. He never slumbers.

Children need to have a similar feeling at home. It's a good idea to always have a light on in the house. One can leave night lights on for young children and porch lights for teenagers who come home late.

The reason we light candles on Shabbos is for the purpose of *shalom bayis*, so that no one should get angry if he bumps against something in the dark. Someone getting up in the middle of the night should be able to see where he's going and feel that someone cares about him enough to leave a light on. The house should never be plunged into darkness.

You can light candles even when there is no halachic obligation. Scented candles also imbue the home with a pleasant fragrance. One nice way to always have light in the house is to have an aquarium with a light. Since fish never sleep, it also provides the reassuring feeling of movement.

Light represents hope, security, and love. There should always be an abundance of these feelings in every home.

Behar

But the seventh year shall be a complete rest for the land.

(Vayikra 25:4)

Our children are like our land. We sow, we nurture, we prune, we tend, and then we hope to reap. But, like the land, our children also need a rest from being reaped and harvested. Children have growth spurts — emotional and spiritual, as well as physical. Sometimes we see lots of growth, and sometimes our children not only do not grow in any obvious way but seem to regress. Many things can trigger this: the birth of a sibling, friction at home, pressure in school. While we should be alert to changes in behavior and be aware of what triggers it, we also need to understand that growing up is difficult, and our children sometimes need a break from the rigors of growing, learning, and achieving. We as parents need to know when to back off and let our children breathe, to chill out. Certainly we should always be there for them if our children seek our help and advice, but sometimes being a parent should be a passive occupation.

You shall hold them as a heritage for your children after you.

(Vayikra 25:46)

While being generous and giving things to others is a virtuous trait, we have to look after our own children's concerns first. In order to retain an inheritance for them, we have to be careful not to squander our wealth and give away our possessions. We have to ensure that all of our children's needs are met before we give to others. Not only is this wise practically, but psychologically. Children should feel that their parents are always looking out for them.

Of course, parents also need to teach their children how to give to others, but this should be something the child does wholeheartedly. Generosity of spirit comes not only from recognizing one's obligation to give but from the feeling that his needs are being taken care of.

Bechukosai

If you follow My decrees and observe My commandments and perform them.

(Vayikra 26:3)

God is very explicit. He tells the people exactly what must be done and what will happen if He is obeyed and what will happen if He isn't. Similarly, children need to know what is expected of them. Rules should be stated clearly, as well as the consequences of violating the rules. Rewards should be offered for following the rules, and there should be consistency in enforcing those rules. But there should be natural consequences for inappropriate behavior, not unwarranted sanctions.

> Punishment connotes retribution and sometimes retaliation. It is attributed to a person in a position of power who judges and decrees. Consequence, on the other hand, is an outcome, a result of another action. It is attributed to a person who is in control of the action. In our case, that person is the child.
>
> *(Make Me, Don't Break Me, p. 153)*

Be as explicit and specific as possible. It's a good idea to involve children in deciding consequences for inappropriate behavior and rewards for fulfilling parental directives. Taking part in the negotiating and deciding motivates them.

> A short time ago a father shared with me the experience of punishing his young son who kept disobeying him by constantly going around the corner. Each time he did so, the father would punish him and tell him not to go around the corner again. But the little boy kept doing it. Finally, after one such punishment, this boy looked at his father with tear-filled eyes and said, "What does 'corner' mean, Daddy?"
>
> *(The 7 Habits of Highly Effective Families, p. 206)*

In *Raising Children to Care* (p. 87), Miriam Adahan raises another point: "It is helpful to think that in most cases it is not lack of respect which causes your child to continue doing what makes him feel good instead of cooperating with your commands, but rather his own inner compulsion to fulfill his need for sensory stimulation." In other words, disobedience isn't the result of disobeying a parent as much as it is giving in to an inner impulse.

BEMIDBAR

מפי עוללים וינקים יסדת עז.

Out of the mouths of babes and sucklings,
You have established strength.

(Tehillim 8:3)

Bemidbar

And they established their genealogy according to
their families, according to their fathers' household.

(Bemidbar 1:18)

Today children who study Torah can tell you the names of
the princes' of each of the twelve tribes, but they can't necessarily
tell you the names of their great-grandparents. While other nations look to the future for guidance, the Jewish people look to
the past. Our role models and leaders have the greatest influence
on our lives, influencing every generation anew.

It's important for children to know their family tree. It gives
them a context, a sense of continuity. The knowledge that they're
part of the history of the Jewish people should be not only intellectual, but they should also have tangible proof, the kind provided by family albums, birth certificates, and letters.

There are valuable lessons to be learned from the past, including our own. Moshe has a history going back to Moshe
Rabbeinu. Esther may have had a great-grandmother who did
tremendous acts of *chesed* or even perhaps saved the lives of
some fellow Jews just like her namesake. Each of us is part of a
genealogy that includes heroes, victims, tzaddikim, villains, and
ordinary people who may have done extraordinary things. Who

we are and who we become has something to do with how, where, and when those ancestors lived their lives. Our family trees have their roots in the cedars of Lebanon, the oak trees of Europe, the maple trees of America, and the pine trees of Jerusalem. Their branches extend wide. Let us embrace them.

Knowing about our family tree has practical as well as spiritual implications. It defines our identity. It tells us whether we are *Ashkenazi*, *Sefardi*, or Yemenite. It gives us important medical information. It explains why we keep certain customs that are geographically related though we've never stepped foot in that country, and it helps us understand things about our own inclinations.

I read a story about a man who had an unusual love of the sea. Eventually he traced his roots back to the seafaring tribe of Zevulun.

It's important to search out and keep family records, "every man according to his families, by his father's household" (*Bemidbar* 2:34), as well as his mother's.

These are the offspring of Aharon and Moshe.... These are the name of the sons of Aharon; the first-born was Nadav and Avihu, Elazar and Isamar.

(Bemidbar 3:1–2)

The Gemara (*Sanhedrin* 19b) asks, if these are the sons of Aharon, why are they listed as the offspring of Moshe? The Gemara infers that if one teaches a child Torah, it is as if he has given birth to him.

While this is encouraging for those people who want to have a lot of children, there's another point to be made. Although one can fulfill the mitzvah to teach one's children Torah by hiring a teacher, a parent should make every effort to personally teach his child at least some Torah. This does not have to apply only to Torah; any area of knowledge or skill that a parent has should be passed on to the child.

Of course, this should be done with patience, good humor, and joy. What we personally can transmit to our children cannot be duplicated by any professional because we infuse our teaching with the special love we have for our children. Our children will better remember these lessons because of their emotional content.

Every firstborn male according to the number of their names, from one month of age and up, according to their numbers, was 22,273.

(Bemidbar 3:43)

Throughout the *Chumash*, the firstborn is accorded special status. While this has many deep philosophical and spiritual reasons, I would like to address a more prosaic one.

The first child is the one that gets the most attention in a family. While this includes positive attention, the firstborn is the one parents make the most mistakes with. He's also the one who gets stuck with the most responsibility. In compensation, the oldest should receive special privileges — allowing him to go to bed later, to be freed of certain duties, to be given extra honor (the first to taste from the Kiddush wine, for example). This will make him feel that it's not so bad to be the oldest.

We always have to keep in mind the status of all family members and make allowances for them: the oldest, the youngest, the "sandwiches." Each child according to his place in the family undergoes his own unique tests. It only stands to reason that he should enjoy special privileges, too. The youngest gets to sleep with mommy, the oldest gets to go on a trip with his class, the middle child gets the piano lessons.

In *Vayishlach*, when Reuven loses his firstborn status because he tampered with his father's bed, Rashi states that he still continued to enjoy certain privileges of the firstborn. There are some things in life that are a child's right, and this includes the right to the love of his parents and his position in the family.

Naso

So shall you bless the children of Israel, saying to
them, "May God bless you and safeguard you. May
God illuminate His countenance for you and be gracious to you. May God lift His countenance to you and
establish peace for you." Let them place My Name
upon the children of Israel, and I shall bless them.

(Bemidbar 6:23–27)

On Friday nights and the nights preceding a festival, parents
bless their children reciting these verses. We should take extra
care in pronouncing the blessing of our children Friday night. In
the *Chumash*, the blessings are written with gaps between them.
This is surely to emphasize the importance of each blessing and
to remind us that they should be said slowly, with emphasis and
kavanah. Our children should feel our immense love for them
with each syllable that we utter.

According to the *Sifri* and others, the first blessing refers to
wealth, the second to the spiritual blessings of Torah knowledge
and inspiration, and the third to God's compassion in granting us
forgiveness and peace whether or not we are deserving. The different objectives of the blessings also refer to our different obligations as parents: our responsibility to provide our children their

material needs, our obligation to instill values in them and teach them Torah, and our duty to be compassionate and loving even when our children are not appreciative or follow erroneous paths. Only by emulating God in these ways can we bestow our blessings on our children and hope for them to be worthy of Hashem's.

The blessings conclude with peace. If there is no peace, nothing else matters. Peace should reign in the Jewish home at all times, not only at candle lighting Friday night.

God said to Moshe, "One leader each day, one leader each day shall they bring their offering for the dedication of the Altar."

(Bemidbar 7:14)

The Torah goes on to record what each representative donated. The Torah, usually so concise, repeats verbatim the offering each tribe made, even though they were exactly the same. This shows that each was uniquely precious to Hashem. That is why He ordered that they be given on separate days – to give honor to each (*Ramban; Chizkuni*).

Often when a child does something he's told that his brother did the same thing when he was his age. But it isn't the *same* thing. It's totally different, because it's being done by a totally different person. Every time a child takes his first step or says his first word, his mother should act as if it's the first time in history a child has ever done this. Parents should react this way to every achievement and contribution a child makes. His achievement is unique and must be regarded as such. If a child gets the feeling that it's no big deal, it's been done before, nothing new under the sun, he'll quickly lose enthusiasm, and his pride in himself will suffer.

Hashem recreates the world every moment. Therefore, anything a child does is for the first time ever.

Beha'aloscha

Did I conceive this entire people, or did I give birth to it, that You say to me, "Carry them in your bosom, as a nurse carries a suckling"?... I alone cannot carry this entire nation, for it is too heavy for me!

(Bemidbar 11:12–14)

Moshe feels the weight of the responsibility of leading the nation, and it is too much to bear. In response, God commands him to gather seventy of the elders and transfers a share of his responsibility over to them. They in turn receive spiritual inspiration from him.

Parents often feel overburdened by the great responsibility parenthood entails. They, too, have people they can turn to for guidance, such as rabbis, guidance counselors, and psychologists, and they have people with whom they can share their burden — teachers, babysitters, counselors, and friends. While it's important to share concerns with knowledgeable people and consider their advice seriously, it's also important to allow other people to give you a reprieve.

However, parents must remember that the same way that Moshe didn't act independently of God and the elders didn't act independently of Moshe, we have to retain a clear hierarchy of responsibility. Parents are the authority regarding their children. They are the ones who make the rules and decisions and give guidance to those trying to help them. Babysitters, caretakers, and teachers must work within the parameters of the parents' *hashkafah*. By the same token, parents would do well to seek guidance in areas where they may be lacking, be it halachah, *hashkafah*, or child development. Parents should rely on their parenting instincts and choose the people from whom they are seeking guidance according to the parenting style with which they feel most comfortable.

Shelach

We were like grasshoppers in our eyes, and so we were in their eyes.

(Bemidbar 13:33)

Even people who are great and powerful sometimes feel insecure. The princes of the Jewish nation, emissaries of God, on a recognizance mission for the whole nation, lacked confidence in themselves and their mission because of their diminutive height in relation to the giants who inhabited the land. Our children who are younger than us, who lack our physical strength (at least till adolescence) and monetary and physical independence, who have little authority, and are significantly smaller than us, feel the same way.

Many parents take advantage of their strength, height, and power to control their children. This is not the way to instill a healthy self-confidence in them. Although we need to maintain our authority, we should not abuse it. Our children are constantly aware of our superiority, but we also need to relate to them at their own level more than just figuratively.

When babies are turning into toddlers, we get down on their hands and knees to baby-proof our homes. While we're down there, it would be a good idea to take a look around and get a "baby's-eye" view of things.

Many psychology books recommend that one spend ten minutes of floor time with one's child each day. Getting down to your child's level, at any age, will make him feel like you're trying to reach him. It must be frustrating for our children to always have to look up to us. When you get down on the floor with your child, show them that what they do there on the floor is important to you.

When your child is young, bend or kneel down so that you're talking to him face to face; don't always pick him up to your level. Look him straight in the eye. This will show you understand him. You'll hear him better, and your words of explanation or comfort will be more readily received.

Make your home child-friendly. Place all medicine, poison, chemicals, alcohol, and the priceless vase you inherited out of reach. The stove should have guards on it or be unplugged when not in use. As soon as your child is old enough, teach him to use it safely. Buy a stool so that washbasins, toilets, cupboard shelves, tables, and bookshelves will be reachable for your child.

Ask your children to help you get things that are too high for you by climbing on a chair. Let them know that there are things that are too hard for you to reach, too. Children love to climb. Encourage them to strive for greater heights (as long as they are protected should they fall), and teach your children that the heights that one should truly strive for are spiritual.

Point out to your children that there are many things smaller than them and teach them, by example, that we should be kind to all of Hashem's creatures, especially those that are smaller than us. Communicate to them in word and deed that the bigger you are, the nicer you have to be.

Korach

Dasan and Aviram went out erect at the entrance to their tents, with their wives, children, and infants.

(Bemidbar 16:27)

The earth opened its mouth and swallowed them and their households, and all the people who were with Korach, and the entire wealth.

(Bemidbar 16:32)

It seems cruel that Dasan and Aviram's small children were destroyed because of their parents' sins. It is true that children often suffer for the sins of their parents, either because they grow up to be sinful, following in their parents' footsteps, and are punished in their own right or because they get caught in the cross fire.

One way to protect our children is to stay clear of sin. By being righteous, we keep evil elements that could be harmful away from our children. If we stay away from criminal elements and stay on the right side of the law, if we are meticulous in our mitzvah observance and try to walk the straight path, we keep ourselves and our family clear of trouble. While trouble often comes

looking for us, it has a harder time finding us if it doesn't recognize us.

If we have found it hard to lead blameless, spotless lives,
there is still hope. Korach's children did *teshuvah* and merited to
have their praises of God included in the book of *Tehillim*. So
even if we have not been fortunate or wise enough to conduct our
lives with the utmost propriety, this does not mean our children
are lost. They may manage to stay on the straight and narrow on
their own. And it is never too late to join them.

Chukas

Then Moshe raised his arm and struck the rock with
his staff twice; abundant water came forth, and the
assembly and the animals drank. Hashem said to
Moshe and to Aharon, "Because you did not believe
in Me to sanctify Me in the eyes of the children of Israel, therefore you will not bring this congregation to
the land that I have given them."

(Bemidbar 20:11−12)

Three lessons of parenting can be gleaned from this incident.
The first is that immediately after Moshe struck the rock, he and
Aharon were told of their punishment. According to the Talmud,
when a child does something wrong, he should be punished
right away or at least informed of his punishment. However, the
Vilna Gaon says that he should also be shown the right thing to
do.

Second, Moshe was punished for striking the rock. He was
supposed to speak to it; instead he struck it, not once but twice.
Moreover, he was expressing his own anger, not God's. In disci-
plining our children, our anger is not supposed to be heartfelt; it
is supposed to be only a facade, expressing our displeasure. As

parents, we are representing God. We are not supposed to strike our children because we are upset. We are not supposed to strike them at all if they may strike us back (which is fairly early on) and certainly not when we feel anger.

Only under extreme circumstances, such as if the child is in danger, has committed a very serious offense, and when we are in control, are we allowed to strike our children, and lightly. In *To Kindle a Soul* (pp. 40–41), Rabbi Kelemen quotes a declaration by the American Academy of Pediatrics, which gives eight negative consequences of spanking children, that it often leads to a cycle of violence.

Finally, according to the Abarbanel and *Midrash Tanchuma*, God's punishment of not allowing Moshe and Aharon to enter the land were really punishments for making the golden calf and dispatching the spies. Although punishment should be meted out immediately, not every infraction need be punished. Sometimes it's better to ignore certain behavior. However, when the misbehavior is cumulative, a parent can take many things into account when deciding on a punishment. Care must be taken not to accumulate too many grievances so as to avoid an explosion of suppressed anger and not to take into account incidents that have already been punished and forgiven.

Israel made a vow to God and said, "If you will deliver this people into my hand, I will consecrate their cities." Hashem heard the voice of Israel.

(Bemidbar 21:2–3)

The people of Israel are usually referred to in the plural, but here they speak as one voice. Families may have internal conflict, but when they are threatened from the outside, they unite against the enemy. Family togetherness is more than just a quaint concept; it's the secret of survival. Nowadays there are many enemies that threaten from the outside. Some are physical threats; others are spiritual dangers. The best way for a family to protect itself is to act as a unit. The more united a family is in its goals, values, and objectives, the more bonded they are and committed to each other, the safer they are from the threats from without.

Balak

How goodly are your tents, O Yaakov, your dwelling places, O Israel.

(Bemidbar 24:5)

Rashi comments that Bilam was inspired by the way the tents were set up in the desert: the tribes dwelt together, and extended families dwelt together, but the way the tents were positioned, with no entrance facing any other, the modesty and privacy of each family was safeguarded. This arrangement ensured that families would be responsible for one another, yet everyone's dignity and rights were preserved.

The sanctity of the family has been severely tested in this past century. Extended families have given way to nuclear families, relatives are scattered across the globe, and the deterioration of the family has led to its members seeking emotional and spiritual support outside its parameters.

The delicate balance that drew a blessing from a prophet who came to curse the people must be maintained. Children need to know that their primary place of support is their family, that their secrets are safe within it, and that there they will always be treated with dignity and respect. Family ties ought to be maintained with relatives who live far away; the extended family should maintain a tradition of assembling at least once a year.

Family members are required to support each other financially, spiritually, and emotionally whenever possible so that they have no need to turn to strangers. Care must be taken to preserve the special history of each family, and the modesty of the home should be upheld.

Modesty helps internalize the concept that there's something worth being modest about. A child who learns modesty — in dress, behavior, and speech — learns that his inner essence is a treasure he must protect.

Pinchas

The daughters of Tzelafchad speak properly. You shall surely give them a possession of inheritance among the brothers of their father, and you shall cause the inheritance of their fathers to pass over to them.

(Bemidbar 27:6–7)

Not only were Tzelafchad's daughters given their father's inheritance, but, according to *Sifri*, this part of the Torah was given through them. They thought of a *chiddush*, so to speak.

Many people who don't know better accuse Judaism of being chauvinistic. Although women certainly have different roles than men, the Torah has always supported the rights, dignity, and intrinsic worth of women. The incident with the daughters of Tzelafchad is only one example.

There have been many attempts to raise boys and girls either completely differently or completely the same. The important thing is that both girls and boys receive attention, respect, rights, and obligations in the family. Girls should be given the opportunity to do mitzvos from which they are not exempted. Women are allowed to make the blessing over the four species, and men are allowed to take *challah*. The love of mitzvos should be encouraged, and the mitzvos of one gender should not be prized over those of the other's.

As Tzelafchad's daughters proved, and set a legal precedent, halachah is not chauvinistic. If a parent is not sure regarding a certain halachah, he should consult a competent halachic authority.

The daughters of Tzelafchad speak properly.

(Bemidbar 27:6)

Rabbi Mordechai Gifter comments on this verse that when someone does something right, we should encourage him by telling him so. Hashem didn't just agree to the women's request; He praised them for speaking properly. So must we do with our own children.

And on the Sabbath day: two male lambs in their first year, unblemished, two tenth *eifah* of fine flour for a meal offering mixed with oil and its libation.

(Bemidbar 28:9)

Sacrifices were part of the daily service during the time of the Beis HaMikdash. Shabbos and holidays were not days off for the *kohanim*.

As parents, we sacrifice a lot for our kids. Not lambs and goats, but time, money and energy. But we complain; we want time off. Being a parent takes lots of hard work. We make sacrifices for our children because, like the *kohanim*, that's our job. There are people who take vacations from their kids — not to be alone with their spouses or to go take care of a sick relative, but vacations from their kids! I'm not saying we don't need a vacation or that some time away from our children is necessarily harmful for them or for us, but when we look forward to time away from our children as a holiday, I think we're missing the point. Begrudging everything we "give up" for our children's well-being goes against the whole idea of parenting. Sure, there are limits, and, sure, we have needs, too, but giving to others is the way we develop love for them.

That's why Hashem mandated sacrifices every day of the year. And that's why children are given to us so vulnerable and helpless — so that we develop our love for them by providing for their needs. This doesn't stop when they can open the fridge and help themselves to a fruit and tie their own shoelaces. It never stops. But with each sacrifice we make to give our children proper nourishment, a roof over their heads, a good education, and the feeling that they're adored, we are raising children who, God willing, will grow up to do the same for another generation of Jewish children. Just like the *kohanim*, this is part of our service to God.

Mattos

They approached him and said, "Pens for the flock shall we build here for our livestock and cities for our small children."

(Bemidbar 32:16)

Build for yourselves cities for your small children and pens for your flock.

(Bemidbar 32:24)

The tribes of Reuven and Gad requested permission to inhabit the land on the other side of the Jordan River. They promised to leave their livestock and children behind and go up with the nation to conquer the land. The syntax of their request shows that their priorities were mixed up. Rashi says that they should not have placed their possessions ahead of their children. Moshe corrects them and tells them to build cities for their children first and then pens for their sheep.

Although it may be easier to build pens for sheep, we have to keep our priorities straight. Our children come before our possessions. If a child breaks something, we should not destroy the dignity and self-esteem of the child. We must not save up to decorate our living rooms if we need the money for our children's education. We should not show off our new Yossi Rosenstein painting to our guests before we show them what Yossi painted at school or say the new *devar Torah* Miriam learned. We mustn't spend extra hours at work at the expense of time we should be spending with our families so we can make payments on the new car. We shouldn't spend hours on our stamp collections or shopping at the mall instead of giving our attention to our children.

A child is not just another possession that happens to be more complex. There are many opportunities in a day to show our children that they mean more to us than our possessions. Things are replaceable; our children are not. Things are lifeless; our children have souls that are eternal. Money is a tool for living; our children are our reason for living. Let us painstakingly guard and cherish our children more ardently than our possessions.

Masei

Moshe wrote their goings forth according to the journeys at the bidding of Hashem, and these were their journeys according to their goings forth.

(Bemidbar 33:2–3)

We take many journeys in our lives, both physical and spiritual. It is wise to document them in order to see where we've been and how far we've come. It's important, too, that we document these journeys for our children so they see where they've been and how far they've come.

Many parents begin documenting and commemorating their children's lives from the time they are born. They record when they got their first tooth, when they took their first step, and they have lots of pictures of their first year. But then it peters out. We need to celebrate every moment of our children's lives, not just the firsts. We need to recall the funny things they did when they were six and the clever *devar Torah* they came up with when they were eight and how nice they looked when they went to their first wedding.

Parents shouldn't be the only ones taking stock and documenting. Children should be encouraged to keep diaries or albums of their achievements. Since children don't always have the time or the means or the ability to express themselves to us or to their teachers, and since disappointments and failures can get blown out of proportion and successes often all but forgotten, writing a diary is a good means of healthy self-expression and it helps the child keep things in perspective.

If a child feels like a failure because he wasn't accepted into a club or he didn't get onto a sports team, the pain won't be so sharp if he opens his diary and reads that the previous year he was voted most likely to succeed. If a child is excited about some event that just happened and no one is home to hear about it, he can express his excitement by writing about it.

Diaries are also good exercises for refining articulation and improving memory. Keeping a diary helps more introverted children open up and extroverted children from opening themselves up too much. Diaries are especially helpful during trying periods when a child needs to work through his thoughts and feelings about a move, an illness, a divorce, a new school, or adolescence.

As parents, we should not pry and ask what the child has written, and certainly we should never read it without the child's permission. We should listen attentively if the child wants to share some of what he wrote. When the child is older, he'll have a keepsake from his childhood that will keep his memories alive.

DEVARIM

למען ידעו דור אחרון, בנים יולדו יקמו ויספרו לבניהם.

So that the last generation may know; children yet to
be born will arise and tell their own children.

(Tehillim 78:6)

Devarim

You are passing through the boundary of your brothers the children of Esav, who dwell in Seir.... You shall not provoke them, for I shall not give you of their land even the right to set foot, for as an inheritance to Esav have I given Mount Seir....

(Devarim 2:4–5)

You shall not distress Moav, and you shall not provoke war with them, for I shall not give you an inheritance from their land, for to the children of Lot have I given Are as an inheritance.

(Devarim 2:9)

This day you shall cross the border of Moav, at Are, and you shall approach opposite the children of Ammon; you shall not distress them, and you shall not provoke them, for I shall not give any of the land of the children of Ammon to you as an inheritance, for to the children of Lot have I given it as an inheritance.

(Devarim 2:18–20)

Children rarely feel they own things. They often have to share everything from their rooms to their clothes. If they don't want to share their most prized possessions, they're threatened that their things will be confiscated.

Some parents threaten that they will cut their children out of their will if they don't listen and do as the parents wish. As they get older, use of the car and other parent-controlled luxuries become a tool of power wielded to manipulate, and provided contingent upon certain behavior.

While children do need to learn to share, and teenagers need to show responsibility in order to earn the right to enjoy certain privileges, everyone from the smallest child to the oldest person needs to feel that certain things belong to him and are under his management. "A person prefers one share of his own possessions to nine identical shares of his friend's" (*Bava Metzia* 38a). Children need to feel that when the time comes they will inherit certain material things from their parents only by virtue of the fact that they are their children. Esav, Lot, and their children did not always do right in the eyes of God, yet God gave them land as an inheritance because He had promised to do so by virtue of their birthright.

Certainly if a child displays good character traits, he should be rewarded. And if a child isn't responsible enough to be trusted with the car, his parents shouldn't risk his life by handing over the keys.

In order to fulfill the dictum of Rabbi Akiva, "What is mine is yours and what is yours is yours," a child has to feel that something really is his. Every person, child or adult, should have a place for his own stuff that, if need be, is guarded by lock and key and is off limits to everyone else. It is wrong for a parent to arbitrarily take things away from children. If a child feels that a parent treats his possessions respectfully, it's likely that he too will treat others' possessions with the same courtesy.

Va'eschanan

Hashem said to me..., "Do not continue to speak to Me further about this matter. Ascend to the top of the cliff and raise your eyes westward, northward, southward, and eastward, and see with your eyes, for you shall not cross this Jordan."

(Devarim 3:26–27)

Moshe's greatest wish was to see Eretz Yisrael. Hashem wouldn't let him enter the land. Instead he told him to ascend the cliff and see the land.

Many times we cannot give our children what they want. But instead of saying an unequivocal no, we can sometimes give our children part of what they want, just as God let Moshe see the land. We can find creative ways of giving our children at least some of their heart's desire, not because we have to give our children everything they want but to show them that we empathize with them and that their needs are important to us.

He chose his offspring after him, and took you out before Himself with His great strength from Egypt, to drive away from before you nations that are greater and mightier than you, to bring you their land as an inheritance, as this very day.

(Devarim 4:37–39)

Everything Hashem did was for the people. He freed them from bondage, He gave them the Torah, and He is about to give them the Land of Israel. Through all this He tolerated disobedience and ingratitude, dissension and complaints. The people still didn't acknowledge that God was good to them and that everything He did was for their benefit.

Our children are a lot like that, too. They don't understand that the things we do, which sometimes seem cruel or unfair, are really for their benefit. We have to make them understand that everything we do is motivated by our intense love for them.

If a child feels loved and understood and most of his perceived needs are met, it will be easier for him to accept and believe that you are withholding something from him or punishing him for his own benefit. However, if you begrudge what you give your children, if you don't make them understand that they are first and foremost in your mind, or if you have ulterior motives when you discipline, then your children will rebel against you. If the children of Israel could rebel against God, Who gave them everything, *kal vachomer* our children will not heed us if our efforts and our concern for them aren't sincere.

Honor your father and your mother, as Hashem, your God, commanded you.

(Devarim 5:16)

God commanded us to honor our parents. He also clarified how to honor them: by not contradicting them, by serving them food and drink, by not sitting in their seat, by not calling them by name, and by taking care of them in their old age. Many parents add all kinds of subclauses to this commandment. When we're educating our children to honor us and we're making parental demands on them, it is best to remember not to demand of them more than God has. We must also remember that honoring parents is for the good of the child, not the parent – "so that your [the child's] days will be lengthened and so that it will be good for you, upon the land that Hashem, your God, gives you" (*Devarim* 5:16).

If your child asks you tomorrow, saying, "What are the testimonies and the decrees and the ordinances that Hashem, our God, commanded you?" you shall say to your child, "We were slaves to Pharaoh in Egypt, and Hashem took us out of Egypt with a strong hand.... And it will be a merit for us if we are careful to perform this entire commandment before Hashem, our God, as He commanded us."

(Devarim 6:20–25)

These verses illustrate two points. Children ask questions about why they have to do certain things. We should answer their questions and not shoo them away as if they shouldn't be bothering us with these questions. Moreover, we should not only answer their questions but answer them in detail.

We also have to point out to them that not only are they required to live by God's commandments, but so are we. "It will be a merit for us." Parents should point out to their children that they themselves must follow the rules they are asking their children to follow. Parents must be role models for their children, behaving in the manner they expect their children to act. When parents practice what they preach, so, most likely, will their children.

Eikev

You should know in your heart that just as a father will chastise his son, so Hashem, your God, chastises you.

(Devarim 8:5)

The Ramban says that just as a father chastises his son to prepare him for the future, so God subjected the people to hardships so that they would appreciate the life waiting for them in Eretz Yisrael.

Sometimes we have to be harsh with our children, not cruel, not unreasonable, but often it's in their best interests to let them tough things out themselves. We could solve all their problems for them and provide everything they need at all times, but that won't build their character or challenge them to rise to the occasion. And it won't provide them with the tools they will need later in life.

When a small child climbs up a slide or a pole, we "spot" him. We stand behind him and catch him if he falls, but we let him climb as high as he is able. We need to do the same thing with Lego towers that fall, with altercations with their friends, with math problems, and with physical, emotional, and moral dilemmas that present themselves to our children on the road to growing up. We need to hold ourselves back from stepping in with the answers and let our children grapple with their problems and find the answers themselves.

This doesn't mean we can't be resource people. We can also give them encouragement, tell them we're behind them, and we can steer them back to the right path when they get too far off course.

Sometimes it's a tough call to know when to interfere and when to step back. A sensitive parent knows when to rush to a toddler's side when he falls and when to stay back and let him get up by himself. We need to retain that sensitivity throughout our children's growing up years so that they grow strong and sure and cheer them on just as we did when they were climbing up the slide.

Sometimes we need to be a bit cruel to be kind. Sometimes we need to let our children nurture themselves. This should not be done at the tender age of three months when a child cries at night, but after many months and years of showing that we are behind our children. God tested the Israelites only after performing many miracles: the plagues, the revelation at Sinai, the water from the rock, the manna, the pillars of cloud and fire. Once our children are sure of our love, and they trust that we'll always be there for them, we can stay a bit in the background.

You shall teach them to your children and discuss them while you sit in your home, while you walk on the way, when you retire, and when you rise.

(Devarim 11:19)

Judaism doesn't recognize that quality time is better than quantity. Parenting is a full-time, twenty-four/seven job. Your children don't learn only when you sit down with them for a few minutes and give them your full attention. Every moment they're in your presence, everything you do, is an opportunity to teach them something. Any time you spend with your children is an opportunity to imbue it with "quality." The more time you spend with your kids, the more opportunity for quality time. You are making an impression on your children each moment you spend with them.

Even what you do when you're away from your children teaches them something. Do you go to a *shiur*, or do you go to play tennis? Do you go out for coffee or do you go to do *chesed*? You are certainly allowed to enjoy a game of tennis or a cup of coffee with friends. But if you do play tennis, is it a friendly game or are you only out to win? If you are going out for coffee, are you speaking *lashon hara* or celebrating someone's birthday? If you're doing *chesed*, are you doing it wholeheartedly or just to show what a good person you are? When you're not with your children, are you thinking of them, calling them, buying them a present? Every moment is precious and must be tapped of its full potential for life, love, and education.

Rav Yechiel Yaakovson talks in his series of tapes on *chinuch* about critical times in the day for parenting. Interestingly, he mentions the times mentioned in the verse. The most critical times for your children are before they go to sleep, when they leave the house, when they come home, and when they get up in the morning.

Rav Yaakovson says that a child must go to sleep feeling calm and content. How he goes to sleep sets the stage for what kind of dreams he is going to have and how the events of the day are processed in his mind. How a child leaves the home and returns to it will determine what feelings about his home he carries with him throughout the day, how happy he is to return home, and how much influence the outside world will have on him. Likewise, the tone for the day is set when he wakes up.

> At these times children are most sensitive to the lack of a mother. The reason for this is that a child lacks self-confidence and needs the warm reassurance and comfort of a mother. When he is getting up or going to sleep, a child feels most insecure, since he is confronting the world or the darkness of sleep. Going to school or coming home are times when the child wishes to share experiences and receive encouragement. Only the mother can fulfill these tasks properly.
>
> *(Beloved Children, p. 66)*

It is no surprise, then, that these times are also when one is required to recite the Shema. If we take care during these times not to rush our children and yell at them, we're creating a welcoming home atmosphere and eliminating a lot of the threat of the outside world. That, along with a prayer, is the best recipe for an emotionally and spiritually healthy child.

> There is an area of family dynamics, however, which can underscore the power and potency of all the rest, while highlighting the need for constant vigilance and preparation: the daily point of reconnection, when each member of the family crosses the threshold coming home. On the one hand, it is an opportunity to find the warmth, comfort, and security of family life. On the other, it is also the time which presents a constant challenge to attend to and be aware of the needs of others.
>
> *(Partners with Hashem, pp. 92–93)*

A child can be put to bed with a lullaby, a tape, a long cuddle, an inspirational story related to some event in his life, and, most important of all, a hug and kiss goodnight (unless the child opposes this).

Besides these critical times during the day, parents should make time to play with their children.

> There is, however, special value in the play of parents and children together. When parents play with a child, they meet him on his level. In fact, truly successful play involves the parent acting in a childlike fashion himself: "...when a man has children, he often makes himself look like a fool to amuse them" (*Bereishis Rabbah* 47). This kind of child-to-child interaction, whereby the adult allows the child within him to resurface, permits parent and child to develop a true rapport of mutual understanding and enjoyment. The youngster is temporarily free of the normal parent-child interactions, which involve so much correction and imply such a lack of acceptance. In the play situation, he is totally relaxed, feeling lovable and acceptable just as he is. He senses the love of his parents and becomes aware of the love he feels for them. This heightened emotional experience extends far beyond the play session itself, coloring the entire nature of the parent-child relationship. The resultant enhanced rapport, or closeness, bonds the child to his parents, increasing his desire to emulate and obey his father and mother.
>
> (*A Delicate Balance, pp. 51–52*)

All these taken together will surely yield much quality interaction between parents and children.

Re'eh

For even their sons and their daughters have they burned in the fire for their gods.

(Devarim 12:31)

God calls the practice of the nations to sacrifice their children to their gods an abomination. Many religions commit horrific acts in the name of their gods. We don't have to go much further than modern-day Palestinians who send their children out to kill and be killed in the name of their beliefs. In Judaism, saving a life defers all but three commandments of the Torah that are considered basic to the survival of the Jewish people.

Sometimes we try to mold our children into what we think they should be. At best, this is like *gezel*, stealing their lives and trying to replace them with our own versions. At worst, it could be sacrifice. There are many children, *Rachmana litzlan*, who perceive Judaism as a punishment. They are coerced and yelled at to do things that are beyond them. These children develop a hatred of our sacred tradition and give it up at the first opportunity. While there are children who go off the *derech* who have been given a perfectly good upbringing, we have to see if the path our children are walking is theirs or ours, or we may turn them off of Judaism.

When a Jewish child first gets a taste of Torah, he's supposed to eat some honey. The feeling that being Jewish is wonderful and learning Torah is sweet should not begin and end with licking honey off the *alef-beis* at cheder. Parents must instill a love of Judaism in their children. When we celebrate the holidays, we must truly *celebrate* them. We have to imbue our children with love of God as well as fear of Him. Doing mitzvos with joy is the preferred method of serving God. Our kids have to internalize that message if they're going to stay within the fold. If children see Judaism as joyful, they look at fasting and refraining from certain activities as a privilege they can't wait to be old enough to do.

There are people who eagerly take on every stringency, but when it comes to *hiddurim*, they don't have the money or it's not their *minhag*. Be *machmir* in *hiddur*. Don't wait for the last minute to put up the sukkah, and don't start putting restrictions on where to eat *chametz* in December. Make an effort to belong to a shul that involves the kids in the service — singing *Adon Olam* and *Anim Zemiros*, taking the crowns off the Torah, and picking up candies from the floor. If your shul doesn't have a candy man, why not become one? If your shul doesn't actively involve children in the service, at least make sure that your shul is child-friendly and makes them feel that they're welcome to participate by offering up their pure prayers.

There's a *minhag* to light a candle on *erev Shabbos* and *chag* for every child in the family. If you don't already do so, it's a good time to start. Your children should know they're the light of your lives and of the nation. (Be careful where you put the candles if you're blessed with a lot of children.)

The joy of Judaism should not be associated by children only with once-a-year events like getting dressed up for Purim and ransoming the *afikoman*. It should be a twenty-four hours a day, seven days a week, every day of the year rejoicing!

If keeping the Torah and mitzvos gives our children their greatest memories, who would ever want to forsake them?

A friend of mine told me a story she heard about a five-year-old girl who asked to go to shul Friday night as she usually did. Her mother wanted to wait for the girl's grandmother to come and take her. The girl fell asleep. When she woke up, she was very upset that she had missed going to shul. To make her feel better, her grandmother took her outside the locked shul, and they sang *Lecha Dodi* together. This is a child who associates going to shul with pleasure, and thanks to her quick-thinking grandmother, she is likely to go on doing so.

Shoftim

Appoint for you judges and guards at all of your gates.

(Devarim 16:18)

The Shelah HaKadosh explains that there are many gates to a man's soul — his eyes, ears, nose, and mouth. The Shelah warns against allowing anything spiritually harmful or unsuitable from passing through those gates.

We must be careful that our impressionable children are not exposed to anything that is inappropriate. We want to keep our children sensitized, not traumatized.

Who is the man who is fearful and fainthearted? Let him go and return to his house, and let him not melt the heart of his fellows, like his heart.

(Devarim 20:8)

During a time of war, certain people were exempt from serving. Among those was someone who feared for his life either because he didn't have enough faith in God or he felt he was not worthy of a miracle to survive.

Fear is a very powerful thing. Sometimes we underestimate

the fears of our children. We brush off the cobwebs of their nightmares and force them to do things they are genuinely afraid of doing. Although we need to encourage them to have faith in themselves and prod them a bit when they hesitate to try new things, we should never force our children to do anything they are genuinely afraid of doing. If it's something they may need to do eventually, like swimming, attending kindergarten, staying alone at home, or getting married, children can either be led into them gradually or the parents can wait until a more propitious time. Throwing a child into deep water either figuratively or literally will only traumatize the child.

Gentle coaxing can be annoying, but forcing a child to do something he's not ready for can leave emotional and psychological scars. It is never necessary to force a child to do something against his will unless it's a matter of life or death, like putting on an oxygen mask or getting an immunization. Since, thank God, few of our life experiences are life-threatening, we can be easy on our children. If God emphasized the danger to an adult going to war against his will even under His promise of protection, then surely we can relax our demands on our own children.

Ki Seitzei

If a man will have two wives, one beloved and one hated, and they bear him sons, the beloved one and the hated one, and the firstborn is the hated one's, then it shall be that on the day he causes his sons to inherit whatever will be his, he cannot give the right of the firstborn to the son of the beloved one ahead of the son of the hated one, the firstborn. Rather, he must recognize the firstborn, the son of the hated one, to give him the double portion in all that is found with him, for he is his initial vigor; to him is the right of the firstborn.

(Devarim 21:15–17)

Ironically this verse is very relevant today. Sometimes children of a first marriage are neglected in favor of the children of the new spouse. While this is sometimes a result of practical difficulties with the first spouse, the children of the first marriage often suffer. They have been replaced in their parent's affections (at least in their own eyes), and they have to cope with this feeling of rejection over and above the trauma of the divorce or the death of a parent.

Noncustodial parents must make it a priority to spend time with their children and maintain a warm and affectionate bond with them. Even though men and women may form new families, the children of the first marriage have a right to both parents' love and attention. While no one is denying that it is sometimes difficult to split oneself between two families, it is a consideration one must bear in mind.

If a man will have a wayward and rebellious son who does not hearken to the voice of his father and the voice of his mother...

(Devarim 21:18)

The fact that this verse immediately follows the ones quoted above and that the parents are spoken of separately ("the voice of his father" and "the voice of his mother") implies that a rebellious son can result from the situation discussed in those verses. It is important, as the Sages teach (*Sanhedrin 71a*), that the mother and father speak in the same voice — have the same values and expectations and not contradict each other. Otherwise the children may become confused and as a result rebellious.

Although the *ben sorer u'moreh*, the rebellious son mentioned in the Torah, is a hypothetical case because the requirements for a child being so defined makes such an occurrence impossible, we can learn an important lesson in unity and harmony. The parents must be similar even in physical appearance (*Sanhedrin 71a*). That could extend to modest or religious dress, style, and expense of the clothes.

All too often parents think nothing of fighting and criticizing each other in front of the children and at the same time think

it is immodest to express words of endearment around them.
It should be the exact opposite!

(Raising Children to Care, p. 210)

Even parents who are divorced can say nice things about
each other without appearing hypocritical:

"Your mom did your hair nicely today."

"I'm glad your father was able to fix your bike."

"I appreciate your mom dropping you guys off on time."

"It was nice of your dad to take you on an outing on Chol
HaMo'ed."

If you build a new house, you shall make a fence for your roof, so that you will not place blood in your house if a fallen one falls from it.

(Devarim 22:8)

The Rambam comments (*Hilchos Rotzei'ach* 11:1–5) that this
includes any dangerous situation, such as a stairwell or swimming pool. Our homes should be safe for our families. As children grow, develop, and change, the kinds of trouble they can
get into changes as well, and so every few months (weeks when
the child is an infant), the house has to be reevaluated for danger.

The ability to consider the outcome of a deed is cited in *Pirkei
Avos* (2:13) as one of the best character traits to have. A parent
must be able to scan a room or area and see what potential dangers lie there. Every home should have a first-aid book and kit as
well as emergency numbers by every phone (police, fire, ambu-
lance, poison control). These numbers can be preprogrammed
into the phone for speed dialing. Every home should have a telephone (I personally think there are safer ways of saving money
than cutting off outgoing calls). Extra sets of keys can be given to

neighbors in case someone gets locked in (or out) by accident. Anyone who is of age to do so should take a first-aid course, and children should be instructed what to do in case a parent loses consciousness. Teaching children to swim is required of parents according to one opinion in the Mishnah.

Children should also be taught to be aware of dangerous situations for the particular area they live in. Someone living in the country should familiarize their children with dangerous plants and animals and give instructions should someone ever be bitten by a snake or scorpion or contract poison ivy. People in the city should teach their children traffic safety and what to do if a stranger follows them.

While avoiding certain topics for reasons of *tznius* is understandable, a child needs to be aware of the fact that there are unstable people who may try to take advantage of his vulnerability. Children of both genders must be taught to recognize danger signals and how to quickly extricate themselves from situations they feel are threatening. This is true if it involves a stranger or someone they feel they should be able to trust. Children need to feel that their parents will protect them from any threat or danger. Never doubt or minimize a child's perceived threat to his safety. Better to err on the side of caution and maintain your children's trust.

The lack of knowing what to do and how to handle such a situation could make their children more vulnerable to attack. If that parent's child is, Heaven forbid, ever victimized, the child would be less likely to come forward and report the incident, since the parents have not given the youngster any indication that such topics may even be discussed. By not discussing the incident the child would then be prevented from receiving the psychological help he or she may need.

(Partners with Hashem, p. 170)

Teaching children about safety in all areas of life gives them the tools to fulfill the mitzvah of *v'nishmartem l'nafshoseichem*, and it teaches them compassion for others and how to ensure the safety of their siblings, friends, and even parents.

The following story happened to someone I know when he was a teenager. He was home alone with his younger sister when a burglar entered their house. He quickly locked himself and his sister in a cupboard. He scared the robber off and no harm was done, but I remember being especially impressed with the fact that his first thought was to save his sister.

You shall not plow with an ox and a donkey together.

(Devarim 22:10)

Rashi comments that this applies to the coupling of different species for any kind of work. Although I'm all for family togetherness, there are situations where putting certain siblings together to work on a project either would be a big mistake because of differences in age or temperament. Parents are like farmers tending their flock. While families should share work and play, results are best attained when we don't mix fire and water.

Remember what Hashem, your God, did to Miriam on the way, when you were leaving Egypt.

(Devarim 24:9)

Many people have purifiers in their homes to purify the air and water filters to cleanse the water. It's equally, if not more important, to always ensure that the speech in our homes is free of *lashon hara*, *rechilus*, and negativity at all times.

You shall not muzzle an ox in its threshing.

(Devarim 25:4)

This commandment appears to be both logical and humane. When the ox is working, it shouldn't be prevented from eating the grain. The home is the threshing ground of our children. It's where they work and grow and play. Therefore there shouldn't be anything around that might tempt children and leave them frustrated because they're not allowed to have it.

This isn't to say that children shouldn't be taught discipline and self-restraint; after all, we are on a higher level than oxen. But sometimes we deny our children things that we can't resist.

A prosaic example could be baking cookies for Shabbos or having the children bake cookies, and we say, "Don't touch them. It will ruin your appetite." If a child does a job, we should let him be the first to enjoy the fruits of his labor. For example, if a kid takes a bike to be fixed, he should be allowed to ride it before anyone else.

These may seem like little things. But, the verse about the ox is interposed between a section about justice and degradation.

Tempting someone and then restraining him from having that which tempts him is degrading as well as frustrating and unjust. We would never think to offer someone who is fasting a drink or a child a new toy and then tell him it isn't for him. Muzzling an ox or restraining a child can be just as dangerous as waving a red flag in front of a bull.

Ki Savo

It will be when you enter the land that Hashem, your God, gives you as an inheritance, and you possess it and dwell in it, that you shall take of the first of every fruit of the ground that you bring in from your land that Hashem, your God, gives you.... You shall come to whomever be the *kohen* in those days.... The *kohen* shall take the basket from your hand....

(Devarim 26:1–4)

One of the nicest wedding *divrei Torah* I have ever heard was from a father who had come with his wife and three children to live in Israel. Their fourth child, a girl, was born in Israel. She had married a *kohen*, and the father said that he had fulfilled the above verse by bringing the first fruits of the land and giving them to the *kohen*.

We no longer have a Beis HaMikdash, *shyibaneh bimheira v'yameinu*. Not all immigrants are going to have daughters to marry off to a *kohen*, and not all of us are going to merit living in Israel before Mashiach comes. However, we can instill in our children a love of the land and a desire to visit, learn, or eventually settle in Israel. Expressing one's love for the Land of Israel and a desire to ultimately live there, God willing, may create a self-fulfilling prophecy so that we will be able to marry off our daughters (or granddaughters) to *kohanim*.

You shall rejoice with all the goodness that Hashem, your God, has given you and your household.

(Devarim 26:11)

Parents often complain that their children don't appreciate all the good they do for them. But gratitude is a learned trait. Do we show appreciation for all the good in our lives, for all the good Hashem does for us? Many people focus on what they don't have. They need to shift their focus. We have so much good in our lives. Even the fact that we're alive is something to be endlessly grateful for.

We can express gratitude for our families, friends, health, homes, jobs, furniture, food. If you're reading this book, it means that (a) you can read, and (b) you can afford to buy it or you have a friend who lent it to you or bought it for you or you have a library or *gemach* you belong to. If you're reading this book, you either have children or grandchildren, are a teacher, or are expecting to be one of the above. There is so much to be grateful for!

We must always be grateful for all the good in our lives. That is the best way to pass on this trait to our children.

Nitzavim

You are standing today, all of you, before
Hashem...all the men of Israel; your small children,
your women, and your proselyte....

(*Devarim* 29:9–10)

According to the Ramban, God wanted the small children to participate in this August event even thought they were too young to legally accept a covenant. What children witness leaves a lasting impression. We often assume children are too young to participate in significant events. The more brisos a child witnesses, the more *divrei Torah* he hears from *gedolim*, the more historic events he experiences, the more he'll assimilate the experiences and incorporate them later in life. Seforno comments on this passage: The future of the Jewish people depends on the education of its children. The building of Jewish schools in a community always takes high priority.

When something really dramatic is going on, something major and life-altering, children are often absent. We think children are too young to be taken to weddings and bar mitzvahs, to see *gedolei hador*, or to witness historic events. The opposite is true. When something major is going on in the family, the community, or the city, the children should be involved and not relegated to the back for when they're older. By the time they're older, these events will make less of an impression on them, and the impact of these events have been lessened.

And you shall choose life so that you will live, you and your offspring.

(Devarim 30:19)

The Torah stresses that the choice of life is not only for the benefit of the one making the choice, but also so that his offspring shall live. This implies that one should choose in such a way that one's offspring as well will be inspired to follow the Torah. If a person obeys the commandments halfheartedly or with the attitude that they are a heavy burden, his children will naturally be reluctant to obey them. But if he studies the Torah and carries out its precepts with joy and pride, his example will carry over to others.

(Rav Moshe Feinstein)

Parents' attitudes help determine their children's attitudes.

Vayeilech

Gather together the people — the men, the women, and the small children.

(Devarim 31:12)

The mother of Yehoshua ben Chananiah, one of the Sages of the Mishnah, used to bring his cradle to the study hall so that he could absorb the sounds of Torah study from infancy. She recognized that the best time to inculcate values in children is from babyhood.

Parents, by virtue of their physical and emotional proximity to their children, are the best people to do this. Thus, Rashi says, for bringing their children to *Hakhel*, parents deserved to be rewarded because they demonstrated to their children that the Torah is precious to them.

There's an old joke about a woman who goes to a psychologist and asks at what age she should start educating her son. The psychologist asks, "How old is the child?"

"A year," the woman answers.

"You're already a year late," he tells her.

The Russian education minister, Ovarov, once asked Rav Chaim Volozhiner when a Jewish child's education begins.

He answered, "Twenty years before he is born."

(My Child, My Disciple, p. 36)

It is unclear at exactly what stage in life children begin to absorb and at what point they can be affected by parental training. There is a great deal of evidence that infants are highly impressionable, and it has been hypothesized that even in intrauterine life the fetus can be affected emotionally as well as physically. Rabbi Shamshon Raphael Hirsch stated that training a child should begin twenty years prior to his birth. What Rabbi Hirsch means is that the Talmudic principle "Correct yourself and then correct others" (*Bava Metzia* 107b) applies to parenting as well as other relationships. *Healthy parenting should begin, not with the focus on the child, but rather with the focus on oneself.*

(Positive Parenting, p. 40)

The Avnei Nezer tells us that the benefit of anything we do is commensurate with our preparation for it. Accordingly, the more we value something, the more extensive our preparation must be.

(My Child, My Disciple, p. 36)

Whether a child's education begins the day he is born, the day he's conceived, twenty years before or several generations before, the basic assumption is that the longer and more intensive the preparation for raising a child, the better the results. This doesn't mean that if you're blessed with a child before you've studied every text on child-rearing, you shouldn't be overjoyed. You may just have to cram.

Education begins from the moment a baby is born. A tiny infant perceives much more about his environment than we

adults attribute to him. The early confrontation with his sur-
roundings influences his behavior and his developing personality. His experiences even as a wee baby become an
integral part of his being.

(Alei Shor, Ma'amar HaChinuch, p. 263,
quoted in Straight from the Heart, p. 21)

Whatever values we want our children to internalize we have
to emphasize from day one. This is the reason children are educated to keep the mitzvos years before they are required to keep
them. If someone learns the wrong thing, it's twice as hard to
undo the habit than if he learns to do it right the first time.

Ha'azinu

Ask your father, and he will tell you, your elders and they will relate it to you.

(Devarim 32:7)

"Elders" refers to grandparents. A careful analysis of the grammar in this verse will indicate that the Hebrew word referring to how a parent will respond connotes a tone of harshness, whereas the word referring to the grandparents' response is one that connotes a much gentler tone of voice.

(Positive Parenting, p. 292)

Grandparents often have more patience and time than parents do. It's a *chesed* of Hashem that grandparents have the chance to rectify the mistakes they made with their children. Children appreciate the love, wisdom, and gentleness they receive from their grandparents. Parents should encourage the contact between the two generations.

Apply your hearts to all the words that I testify against you today with which you are to instruct your children, to be careful to perform all the words of this Torah.

(Devarim 32:46)

These are among Moshe's last words. Last words bear the greatest significance. Instructing our children, the future of the nation, is Moshe's parting command to the nation. That is our greatest obligation — to create another generation of Torah-observant, God-fearing Jews.

Vezos HaBerachah

And this is the blessing that Moshe, the man of God, bestowed upon the children of Israel before his death.

(Devarim 33:1)

Moshe does three things before his death that contain a lesson for all parents: he appoints a leader in his place in view of the nation, he blesses the nation, and he takes his leave.

Parenting doesn't stop after we die. We have to make sure we leave our affairs in order, make a will, appoint responsible people to take charge of our estate, take care of any unfinished business, and, finally, give our children our blessing.

Many parents leave debts and unsettled legal issues for their children to deal with. Others, worse still, leave unresolved emotional issues so that the child either begrudges the parent or feels guilty for the rest of his life. When our children come into our lives, they do so with a clean slate. When we leave them at 120, like Moshe Rabbeinu we should leave them with a clean slate. Before leaving this world, we must ask our children's forgiveness, forgive our children, and bless them.

Even after our children are grown we have certain responsibilities to make sure our children are taken care of. We can make a will when our children are still young and update it as appropriate. Leaving them a legacy — financial, emotional, and spiritual — is our last duty as parents in this world.

We must ensure that the last words our children hear from us are words of blessing. Since we don't know when is the last time we will see our children, it's best to always leave them with words of blessing, praise, and love.

Moshe died by a divine kiss, as it says, "*al pi Hashem* — by the mouth of Hashem." The last thing Moshe experienced in this world was a kiss from his Father in Heaven. Our children should experience our affection for them until we are 120 years old.

May we all merit to raise children and grandchildren who bring *nachas* to us and to Hashem in good health with patience and wisdom till 120.

SPECIAL PRAYERS

Prayer is one of the most powerful forces in raising children. A Heavenly decree can be changed through prayer. The following are a list of prayers parents say for their children. Prayers need to be adjusted for gender and number of children.

ברכת הבנים

לבן : יְשִׂמְךָ אֱלֹהִים כְּאֶפְרַיִם וְכִמְנַשֶּׁה :

לבת : יְשִׂמֵךְ אֱלֹהִים כְּשָׂרָה רִבְקָה רָחֵל וְלֵאָה :

יְבָרֶכְךָ ה׳ וְיִשְׁמְרֶךָ. יָאֵר ה׳ פָּנָיו אֵלֶיךָ וִיחֻנֶּךָּ. יִשָּׂא ה׳ פָּנָיו אֵלֶיךָ
וְיָשֵׂם לְךָ שָׁלוֹם :

נוסח של ר׳ יהודה הנקין לבת : יְשִׂמֵךְ אֱלֹהִים כְּרָחֵל וְלֵאָה אֲשֶׁר
בָּנוּ שְׁתֵּיהֶן אֶת בֵּית יִשְׂרָאֵל :

Blessing of Children on Friday Night

For a boy: May God make you like Efraim and Menasheh.

For a girl: May God make you like Sarah, Rivkah, Rachel, and Leah.

May God bless you and safeguard you. May God illuminate His countenance for you and be gracious to you. May God turn His countenance to you and establish peace for you.

Rabbi Yehudah Henkin added his own nusach for the berachah for girls:

May God make you like Rachel and Leah who built the House of Israel.

(Based on Megillas Rus)

An extended version of this prayer is often recited on erev Yom Kippur and is found in many machzors.

תפילה לאחר הדלקת נרות

לאחר הדלקת הנרות לומר :

יְהִי רָצוֹן מִלְפָנֶיךָ, ה׳ אֱלֹהֵינוּ וֵאלֹהֵי אֲבוֹתֵינוּ, שֶׁיִבָּנֶה בֵּית הַמִּקְדָּשׁ בִּמְהֵרָה בְיָמֵינוּ, וְתֵן חֶלְקֵנוּ בְּתוֹרָתֶךָ, וְשָׁם נַעֲבָדְךָ בְּיִרְאָה כִּימֵי עוֹלָם וּכְשָׁנִים קַדְמוֹנִיּוֹת. וְעָרְבָה לַה׳ מִנְחַת יְהוּדָה וִירוּשָׁלָיִם, כִּימֵי עוֹלָם וּכְשָׁנִים קַדְמוֹנִיּוֹת :

תפילה לאחר הדלקת הנרות :

יְהִי רָצוֹן מִלְפָנֶיךָ, ה׳ אֱלֹהֵינוּ וֵאלֹהֵי אֲבוֹתֵינוּ, שֶׁתְּחוֹנֵן אוֹתִי (וְאֶת בַּעְלִי), וְאֶת כָּל קְרוֹבַי, וְתִתֵּן לָנוּ וּלְכָל יִשְׂרָאֵל חַיִּים טוֹבִים וַאֲרוּכִים, וְתִזְכְּרֵנוּ בְּזִכְרוֹן טוֹבָה וּבְרָכָה, וְתִפְקְדֵנוּ בִּפְקֻדַּת יְשׁוּעָה וְרַחֲמִים, וְתַשְׁכֵּן שְׁכִינָתְךָ בֵּינֵינוּ, וְזַכֵּנוּ לְגַדֵּל בָּנִים וּבְנֵי בָנִים חֲכָמִים וּנְבוֹנִים, אוֹהֲבֵי ה׳, יִרְאֵי אֱלֹהִים, אַנְשֵׁי אֱמֶת, זֶרַע קֹדֶשׁ, בַּה׳ דְּבֵקִים, וּמְאִירִים אֶת הָעוֹלָם בַּתּוֹרָה וּבְמַעֲשִׂים טוֹבִים וּבְכָל מְלֶאכֶת עֲבוֹדַת הַבּוֹרֵא. אָנָּא, שְׁמַע אֶת תְּחִנָּתִי בִּזְכוּת שָׂרָה וְרִבְקָה רָחֵל וְלֵאָה אִמּוֹתֵינוּ, וְהָאֵר נֵרֵנוּ שֶׁלֹּא יִכְבֶּה לְעוֹלָם וָעֶד, וְהָאֵר פָּנֶיךָ וְנִוָּשֵׁעָה, אָמֵן :

Prayer after Lighting Candles

After lighting the candles, it is customary to say:

May it be Your will, Eternal, our God and God of our fathers, that the Beis HaMikdash be soon rebuilt in our days, and give us our portion in Your Torah, so that we may serve You there with reverence as in the days of the past and as in former years.

A prayer following candle lighting:

May it be Your will, Eternal, our God and God of our fathers, that You show favor to me (my husband) and all my relatives. Grant us and all Israel a good and long life, and remember us with a favorable memory and blessing. Recall us with a recollection of salvation and mercy, and cause Your presence to dwell among us. Make us worthy of raising wise and understanding children and grandchildren, who love the Eternal and are God-fearing and truthful, holy offspring who will cling to the Eternal and illuminate the world with Torah, good deeds, and all manner of service to the Creator. Please accept my plea in the merit of our mothers Sarah, Rivkah, Rachel, and Leah, and cause our light to glow brightly forever. Let Your countenance shine, so that we may be saved, Amen.

תפילת אבות על בנים

רִבּוֹנוֹ שֶׁל עוֹלָם זַכֵּנוּ שֶׁיִּהְיוּ בָּנֵינוּ מְאִירִים בַּתּוֹרָה (מי שאין בנים אומר: זַכֵּנוּ לְהוֹלִיד בָּנִים טוֹבִים מְאִירִים בַּתּוֹרָה) וְיִהְיוּ בְּרִיאִים בְּגוּפָם וּבְשִׂכְלָם בַּעֲלֵי מִדּוֹת טוֹבוֹת עוֹסְקִים בַּתּוֹרָה לִשְׁמָהּ. וְתֶן לָהֶם חַיִּים אֲרוּכִים וְטוֹבִים. וְיִהְיוּ מְמֻלָּאִים בְּתוֹרָה וּבְחָכְמָה וּבְיִרְאַת שָׁמַיִם. וְיִהְיוּ אֲהוּבִים לְמַעֲלָה וְנֶחְמָדִים לְמַטָּה. וְתַצִּילֵם מֵעַיִן הָרַע וּמִיֵּצֶר הָרַע וּמִכָּל מִינֵי פֻּרְעָנִיּוֹת. וְיִהְיוּ לָהֶם חוּשִׁים בְּרִיאִים לַעֲבוֹדָתֶן. וְזַכֵּנִי (ואת אשתי) (ואת בעלי) בְּרַחֲמֶין הָרַבִּים שֶׁתְּמַלֵּא מִסְפַּר יָמֵינוּ עַד מְלֹאת שִׁבְעִים שָׁנָה וְיוֹתֵר בְּטוֹב וּבִנְעִימִים וְאַהֲבָה וְשָׁלוֹם. וְנִזְכֶּה לְגַדֵּל כָּל אֶחָד מִבָּנֵינוּ וְכָל אַחַת מִבְּנוֹתֵינוּ לַתּוֹרָה וּלְחֻפָּה וּלְמַעֲשִׂים טוֹבִים. וְתַזְמִין לָהֶם זִיווּגָם בְּנָקֵל וְלֹא יוֹדְחוּ לִפְנֵי אֲחֵרִים חַס וְשָׁלוֹם. וּבְרֵךְ מַעֲשֵׂה יָדֵינוּ לִיתֵּן לָהֶם מַהֵר וּמַתָּן בְּעַיִן יָפָה. וְנוּכַל לְקַיֵּם כָּל מַה שֶׁאָנוּ מַבְטִיחִים בְּלֹא נֶדֶר לִיתֵּן לָהֶם. וּלְהַשִּׂיאָם עִם זִיווּגָם בִּימֵי הַנְּעוּרִים בְּנַחַת וּבְרֶוַח וּבְשִׂמְחָה. וְיוֹלִידוּ בָּנֵינוּ וּבְנוֹתֵינוּ בָּנִים טוֹבִים צַדִּיקִים זוֹכִים וּמְזַכִּים לְכָל יִשְׂרָאֵל. וְיִהְיוּ בָּנֵינוּ וּבְנוֹתֵינוּ חַיִּים וְקַיָּמִים בַּעֲבוֹדָתֶן וּבְתוֹרָתֶן וּבְיִרְאָתֶן לְאֹרֶךְ יָמִים וְשָׁנִים טוֹבוֹת. וְיִתְרַבּוּ צֶאֱצָאֵיהֶם עַד סוֹף כָּל הַדּוֹרוֹת. וְלֹא יִתְחַלֵּל שִׁמְךָ הַגָּדוֹל עַל יָדֵינוּ וְלֹא עַל יְדֵי זַרְעֵנוּ חַס וְשָׁלוֹם. וּמַלֵּא כָּל מִשְׁאֲלוֹת לִבֵּנוּ לְטוֹבָה בִּבְרִיאוּת וְהַצְלָחָה וְכָל טוּב. וְנִזְכֶּה לְהַגְדִּיל כְּבוֹד שִׁמְךָ הַגָּדוֹל וּכְבוֹד תּוֹרָתֶן אָנוּ וְזַרְעֵנוּ וְזֶרַע זַרְעֵנוּ תָּמִיד. אָמֵן כֵּן יְהִי רָצוֹן. יִהְיוּ לְרָצוֹן אִמְרֵי פִי וְהֶגְיוֹן לִבִּי לְפָנֶיךָ, ה' צוּרִי וְגוֹאֲלִי:

Prayer for One's Children

Master of the universe: May we be worthy of having children who will radiate Torah, who will be healthy physically and mentally and of fine character. May they occupy themselves in Torah for its own sake. Grant them a long and good life. Let them be filled with Torah, wisdom, and the fear of Heaven, and be beloved to You and their fellow human beings. Spare them from an evil eye, from the evil inclination, and from any distress. May they have alert senses with which to serve You. In Your great mercy grant me and my wife (or: husband) a life of seventy or more good and pleasant years, filled with love and peace. May we merit to raise each of our sons and daughters to Torah, marriage, and good deeds. Enable them to find their match with ease, so they won't lose out to someone else, God forbid. Bless us with the ability to provide them with abundant dowries, to fulfill all our promises to them, and to marry them off young, contentedly, generously, and happily. Give our sons and daughters good and righteous children who will be a credit to all Israel, and may they continue to serve and fear You and to live by Your Torah for many good years, and be blessed with many descendants. May we and our progeny never desecrate Your great Name. Fulfill all our hearts' requests for the good, in health, success, and goodness. May we, our children, and our children's children enhance the honor of Your great Name and Your Torah forever, Amen and so may it be. May the words of my mouth and the thoughts of my heart be pleasing before You, Eternal, my Rock and my Redeemer.

תפילת אבות ואמהות לערב ראש חודש סיון לחינוך ילדים

מאת השל״ה הקדוש

חל עלינו חובת התפילה ובקשה להש״י בכל צרכינו כי הכל מאתו יתברך. על כן בכל מה שיצטרך האדם בכל עת ובכל שעה ירגיל על לשונו תפילה קצרה להשליך על ה׳ יהבו, ובעת הפעולה יאמר בכל צרכיו לשם יחוד קב״ה ושכינתיה רבון העולמים הצליח דרכי כי מאתך הכל וכו׳. וביותר צריך זירוז להתפלל שיהיה לו זרע כשר עד עולם. ואגב כל צרכיהם וזיווגם מה׳ יצא הדבר. ולבי אומר שעת רצון לתפילה זו בערב ר״ח סיון הוא החודש שבו נתנה התורה ואז נקראים בנים לה׳ אלהינו. וראוי לישב בתענית ביום ההוא הוא ואשתו ויתעוררו בתשובה ויתקנו כל עניני הבית איסור והיתר וטומאה וטהרה וכל העניינים, ויתנו צדקה לענײם הגונים ואם אפשר לבעל להתענות אז הפסקה מה טוב ומה נעים. ועכ״פ יהיה תענית גמור בכל דיני תענית ציבור. וזה הנוסחא של התפילה:

אַתָּה הוּא ה׳ אֱלֹהֵינוּ עַד שֶׁלֹא בָּרָאתָ הָעוֹלָם, וְאַתָּה הוּא אֱלֹהֵינוּ מִשֶּׁבָּרָאתָ הָעוֹלָם, וּמֵעוֹלָם וְעַד עוֹלָם אַתָּה אֵל. וּבָרָאתָ עוֹלָמְךָ בְּגִין לְאִשְׁתְּמוֹדַע אֱלֹהוּתָךְ בְּאֶמְצָעוּת תּוֹרָתְךָ הַקְּדוֹשָׁה כְּמוֹ שֶׁאָמְרוּ רז״ל בְּרֵאשִׁית בִּשְׁבִיל תּוֹרָה, וּבִשְׁבִיל יִשְׂרָאֵל כִּי הֵם עַמְּךָ וְנַחֲלָתְךָ

Prayer for the Day before Rosh Chodesh Sivan for the Education of Children

by the Shelah HaKadosh

We must pray to God for all our needs, because everything comes from Him. Therefore, anytime we need something, we should train ourselves to recite a short prayer and cast our burden upon God. Before doing anything, we should say that "it is for the sake of unifying the Holy One, blessed is He, and His Presence; Master of the Universe, help me succeed, for everything is from You." One must especially pray to have proper descendants exclusively, and that God provide them with all their needs and appropriate marriage partners. I believe that the day before Rosh Chodesh Sivan is a most opportune time for this prayer, because the Torah was given in that month, and we are then called "children of the Eternal, our God." It is appropriate for a husband and wife to fast on that day, to repent, and to set their house in order, as far as religious deficiencies are concerned. They should give charity, and they should fast, keeping all the laws of a public fast, if possible.

You have been the Eternal, our God, before You created the world and You are the Eternal, our God, since You created the world, and You are God forever. You created Your world so that Your Divinity should become revealed through Your holy Torah, as

אֲשֶׁר בָּחַרְתָּ בָּהֶם מִכָּל הָאֻמּוֹת וְנָתַתָּ לָהֶם תּוֹרָתְךָ הַקְּדוֹשָׁה וְקֵרַבְתָּם לְשִׁמְךָ הַגָּדוֹל. וְעַל קִיּוּם הַתּוֹרָה בָּא לָנוּ מִמְּךָ ה' אֱלֹהֵינוּ שְׁנֵי צִוּוּיִם: כָּתַבְתָּ בְּתוֹרָתְךָ פְּרוּ וּרְבוּ, וְכָתַבְתָּ בְּתוֹרָתְךָ וְלִמַּדְתֶּם אֹתָם אֶת בְּנֵיכֶם. וְהַכַּוָּנָה בִּשְׁתֵּיהֶן אַחַת כִּי לֹא לְתֹהוּ בְּרָאתָ כִּי אִם לָשֶׁבֶת וְלִכְבוֹדְךָ בְּרָאתָ יָצַרְתָּ אַף עָשִׂיתָ כְּדֵי שֶׁנִּהְיֶה אֲנַחְנוּ וְצֶאֱצָאֵינוּ וְצֶאֱצָאֵי כָּל עַמְּךָ בֵּית יִשְׂרָאֵל יוֹדְעֵי שְׁמֶךָ וְלוֹמְדֵי תוֹרָתֶךָ:

וּבְכֵן אָבוֹא אֵלֶיךָ ה' מֶלֶךְ מַלְכֵי הַמְּלָכִים וְאַפִּיל תְּחִנָּתִי וְעֵינַי לְךָ תְלוּיוֹת עַד שֶׁתְּחָנֵּנִי וְתִשְׁמַע תְּפִלָּתִי לְהַזְמִין לִי בָּנִים וּבָנוֹת, וְגַם הֵם יִפְרוּ וְיִרְבּוּ הֵם וּבְנֵיהֶם וּבְנֵי בְנֵיהֶם עַד סוֹף כָּל הַדּוֹרוֹת לְתַכְלִית שֶׁהֵם וַאֲנַחְנוּ כֻּלָּנוּ יַעַסְקוּ בְּתוֹרָתְךָ הַקְּדוֹשָׁה לִלְמֹד וּלְלַמֵּד לִשְׁמֹר וְלַעֲשׂוֹת וּלְקַיֵּם אֶת כָּל דִּבְרֵי תַלְמוּד תּוֹרָתֶךָ בְּאַהֲבָה. וְהָאֵר עֵינֵינוּ בְּתוֹרָתֶךָ וְדַבֵּק לִבֵּנוּ בְּמִצְוֹתֶיךָ לְאַהֲבָה וּלְיִרְאָה אֶת שְׁמֶךָ:

אָבִינוּ אָב הָרַחֲמָן תֵּן לְכֻלָּנוּ חַיִּים אֲרוּכִים וּבְרוּכִים. מִי כָמוֹךָ אָב הָרַחֲמָן זוֹכֵר יְצוּרָיו לְחַיִּים בְּרַחֲמִים. זָכְרֵנוּ לְחַיִּים נִצְחִיִּים כְּמוֹ שֶׁהִתְפַּלֵּל אַבְרָהָם אָבִינוּ "לוּ (יִשְׁמָעֵאל) יִחְיֶה לְפָנֶיךָ" וּפֵרְשׁוּ רַבּוֹתֵינוּ זִכְרוֹנָם לִבְרָכָה, בְּיִרְאָתֶךָ:

כִּי עַל כֵּן בָּאתִי לְבַקֵּשׁ וּלְהִתְחַנֵּן וּלְהִתְחַנֵּן מִלְּפָנֶיךָ שֶׁיִּהְיֶה זַרְעִי זֶרַע כָּשֵׁר. וְאַל תִּמָּצֵא בִי וּבְזַרְעִי וּבְזֶרַע זַרְעִי עַד עוֹלָם שׁוּם פְּסוּל וּשְׁמָץ. אַךְ שָׁלוֹם וֶאֱמֶת וְטוֹב וְיָשָׁר בְּעֵינֵי אֱלֹהִים וּבְעֵינֵי אָדָם. וְיִהְיוּ בַּעֲלֵי תוֹרָה, מָארֵי מִקְרָא, מָארֵי מִשְׁנָה, מָארֵי תַלְמוּד, מָארֵי רָזָא, מָארֵי מִצְוָה, מָארֵי גוֹמְלֵי חֲסָדִים, מָארֵי מִדּוֹת תְּרוּמִיּוֹת. וְיַעַבְדוּךָ בְּאַהֲבָה וּבְיִרְאָה פְּנִימִית וְלֹא יִרְאָה חִיצוֹנִית. וְתֵן לְכָל גּוּיָה וּגְוִיָּה מֵהֶם דֵּי מַחְסוֹרָהּ בְּכָבוֹד. וְתֵן לָהֶם בְּרִיאוּת וְכָבוֹד וְכֹחַ. וְתֵן לָהֶם קוֹמָה וְיוֹפִי וְחֵן וָחֶסֶד. וְיִהְיֶה אַהֲבָה וְאַחְוָה וְשָׁלוֹם בֵּינֵיהֶם. וְתַזְמִין לָהֶם זִוּוּגִים הֲגוּנִים מִזֶּרַע תַּלְמִידֵי חֲכָמִים מִזֶּרַע צַדִּיקִים, וְגַם הֵם זִוּוּגָם יִהְיֶה כְּמוֹתָם בְּכָל אֲשֶׁר הִתְפַּלַּלְתִּי עֲלֵיהֶם כִּי זִכָּרוֹן אֶחָד עוֹלֶה לְכָאן וּלְכָאן:

our Sages expounded on the first word therein, and for Israel, for they are Your people and Your inheritance whom You have chosen from among all nations. You have given them Your holy Torah and drawn them towards Your great Name. These two commandments are "Be fruitful and multiply," and "You shall teach them to Your children." Their purpose is that You did not create the world to be empty, but to be inhabited, and that it is for Your glory that You created, fashioned, and perfected it, so that we, our offspring, and all the descendants of Your people Israel will know Your Name and study Your Torah.

Thus I entreat You, O Eternal, supreme King of kings. My eyes are fixed on You until You favor me, and hear my prayer, and provide me with sons and daughters who will also be fruitful and multiply, they and their descendants unto all generations, in order that they and we may all engage in the study of Your holy Torah, to learn and to teach, to observe, to do, and to fulfill with love all the words of Your Torah's teachings. Enlighten our eyes in Your Torah, and attach our heart to Your commandments, to love and revere Your Name

Our Father, compassionate Father, grant us all a long and blessed life. Who is like You, compassionate Father, Who in compassion remembers His creatures for life! Remember us for eternal life, as our forefather Avraham prayed, "If only Yishmael would live before You," which the Sages interpreted as "...live in reverence of You."

For this I have come to appeal and plead before You, that my offspring and their descendants be proper, and that You find no imperfection or disrepute in me or them forever. May they be people of peace, truth, goodness, and integrity in the eyes of God and man. Help them to become practiced in Torah, accomplished in Scriptures, Mishnah, Talmud, Kabbalah, mitzvos, kindness, and good attributes, and to serve You with an inner love and reverence, not merely outwardly. Provide every one of them with their needs with honor, and give them health, honor and strength, good bearing and appearance, grace and loving-kindness. May love and brotherhood

אַתָּה ה' יוֹדֵעַ כָּל תַּעֲלוּמוֹת וּלְפָנֶיךָ נִגְלוּ מִצְפּוּנֵי לִבִּי. כִּי כַוַּנָתִי בְּכָל אֵלֶּה לְמַעַן שִׁמְךָ הַגָּדוֹל וְהַקָּדוֹשׁ וּלְמַעַן תּוֹרָתְךָ הַקְּדוֹשָׁה. עַל כֵּן עֲנֵנִי ה' עֲנֵנִי בַּעֲבוּר הָאָבוֹת הַקְּדוֹשִׁים אַבְרָהָם יִצְחָק וְיַעֲקֹב. וּבִגְלַל אָבוֹת תּוֹשִׁיעַ בָּנִים לִהְיוֹת הָעֲנָפִים דּוֹמִים לְשָׁרְשָׁם בַּעֲבוּר דָּוִד עַבְדְּךָ רֶגֶל רְבִיעִי בַּמֶּרְכָּבָה הַמְשׁוֹרֵר בְּרוּחַ קָדְשֶׁךָ:

שִׁיר הַמַּעֲלוֹת אַשְׁרֵי כָּל יְרֵא ה' הַהֹלֵךְ בִּדְרָכָיו: יְגִיעַ כַּפֶּיךָ כִּי תֹאכֵל אַשְׁרֶיךָ וְטוֹב לָךְ: אֶשְׁתְּךָ כְּגֶפֶן פֹּרִיָּה בְּיַרְכְּתֵי בֵיתֶךָ בָּנֶיךָ כִּשְׁתִלֵי זֵיתִים סָבִיב לְשֻׁלְחָנֶךָ: הִנֵּה כִי כֵן יְבֹרַךְ גָּבֶר יְרֵא ה': יְבָרֶכְךָ ה' מִצִּיּוֹן וּרְאֵה בְּטוּב יְרוּשָׁלָיִם כֹּל יְמֵי חַיֶּיךָ: וּרְאֵה בָנִים לְבָנֶיךָ שָׁלוֹם עַל יִשְׂרָאֵל:

אָנָּא ה' שׁוֹמֵעַ תְּפִלָּה. יְקַיַּם הַפָּסוּק וַאֲנִי זֹאת בְּרִיתִי אוֹתָם אָמַר ה' רוּחִי אֲשֶׁר עָלֶיךָ וּדְבָרַי אֲשֶׁר שַׂמְתִּי בְּפִיךָ לֹא יָמוּשׁוּ מִפִּיךָ וּמִפִּי זַרְעֲךָ וּמִפִּי זֶרַע זַרְעֲךָ אָמַר ה' מֵעַתָּה וְעַד עוֹלָם. יִהְיוּ לְרָצוֹן אִמְרֵי פִי וְהֶגְיוֹן לִבִּי לְפָנֶיךָ ה' צוּרִי וְגוֹאֲלִי:

reign among them. Provide them with suitable marriage partners of scholarly and righteous parentage who will also be blessed with all that I have asked for my own descendants, since they will share the same fate.

You, the Eternal, know everything that is concealed, and to You all my heart's secrets are revealed. For all my intention concerning the above is for the sake of Your great and holy Name and Torah. Therefore, answer me, O Eternal, answer me in the merit of our holy forefathers Avraham, Yitzchak, and Yaakov. For the sake of the fathers save the children, so the branches will be like the roots. For the sake of Your servant, David, who is the fourth part of Your Chariot, who sings with Divine inspiration.

A song of ascents. Fortunate is everyone who fears the Eternal, who walks in His ways. When you eat of the toil of your hands, you are fortunate, and good will be yours. Your wife is like a fruitful vine in the inner chambers of your home; your children are like olive shoots around your table. Look! So is blessed the man who fears the Eternal. May the Eternal bless you from Zion, and may you see the good of Jerusalem all the days of your life. May you see your children's children, peace upon Israel.

Please, O Eternal, Who listens to prayer, may the following verse be fulfilled in me: " 'As for Me,' said the Eternal, 'this My covenant shall remain their very being; My spirit, which rests upon you, and My words which I have put in your mouth, shall not depart from your mouth, nor from the mouths of your children, nor from the mouths of your children's children,' said the Eternal, 'from now to all eternity.' " May the words of my mouth and the thoughts of my heart be pleasing before You, Eternal, my Rock and my Redeemer.

תפילה להצלחה בתורה

יְהִי רָצוֹן מִלְּפָנֶיךָ, שֶׁתְּרַחֵם עַל (פב״פ) וְתַהֲפֹךְ אֶת לְבָבוֹ לְאַהֲבָה וּלְיִרְאָה שְׁמֶךָ, וְלִשְׁקֹד בְּתוֹרָתְךָ הַקְּדוֹשָׁה, וְתָסִיר מִלְּפָנָיו כָּל הַסִּבּוֹת הַמּוֹנְעוֹת אוֹתוֹ מִשְּׁקִידַת תּוֹרָתְךָ הַקְּדוֹשָׁה, וְתָכִין אֶת כָּל הַסִּבּוֹת הַמְּבִיאוֹת לְתוֹרָתְךָ הַקְּדוֹשָׁה, כִּי אַתָּה שׁוֹמֵעַ תְּפִלָּה בְּרַחֲמִים, בָּרוּךְ אַתָּה ה׳ שׁוֹמֵעַ תְּפִלָּה:

Prayer for Success in Torah

May it be Your will to have mercy on (name) and to turn his heart to love and to be in awe of Your Name, and to diligently study Your holy Torah. Remove from before him any obstacles that prevent him from doing so and present him with all the incentives to study it. For You hear prayer with compassion. Blessed are You, Eternal, Who hears prayer.

(Chazon Ish)

It is a segulah to read chapter 1 of Shmuel after candle lighting Friday night.

It is recommended to read Iggeres HaRambam to your children once a week.

Glossary

Adam karov l'atzmo — A person understands himself.

Adon Olam — Literally, "Master of the universe"; a prayer.

alef-beis — Hebrew alphabet.

Anim Zemiros — Literally, "pleasant melodies"; the opening verse of the Song of Glory.

Aron — Ark.

ba'al teshuvah — Penitent.

ba'alebatim — Working religious Jews.

baruch Hashem — Literally, "God should be blessed"; thank God.

Beis HaMikdash — The Holy Temple.

ben sorer u'moreh — Rebellious child described in Scripture.

berachah — Blessing.

b'ezras Hashem — With God's help; God willing.

binah yeseirah — Added insight.

bli ayin hara — Without the evil eye.

bli neder — Without promising.

bubby — Grandmother.

chag — Festival.

chametz — Leaven.

chas v'shalom — God forbid.

cheder — Boys' elementary school.

chesed — Acts of lovingkindness.

chiddush — New Torah insight.

Chol HaMo'ed — The intermediary days of a festival.

Chumash — Five books of the Torah.

chumra — Halachic stringency.

daven — Pray.

davka — On purpose.

derech — Path.

derech eretz — Good manners; proper conduct.

devar Torah (pl. *divrei Torah*) — Torah discourse.

erev — Eve.

esrog — Citron; one of the four spcies that are blessed on Sukkos.

gedolim; *gedolei hador* — Leaders of the generation.

gemach — Free-loan fund.

Gemara — Talmud.

HaKadosh Baruch Hu — Literally, "the Holy One, blessed is He," referring to God.

Hakhel — Gathering of the entire nation when the king reads the Torah.

halachah — Jewish law.

hashkafah — Outlook.

Havdalah — Prayer recited at the conclusion of the Sabbath.

hiddur — Beautification.

ilui neshamah — Elevating the soul through a good deed or commandment done in the deceased's memory.

kal vachomer — Even more so.

kavanah — Concentration.

kedushah — Holiness.

kibbud av va'em — Honoring one's father and mother.

Kiddush — Blessing recited over wine on the Sabbath and festivals.

kohen (pl. *kohanim*) — Priest; descendant of Aaron whose task is to serve in the Holy Temple.

kohen gadol — High priest.

lashon hara — Evil speech.

Lecha Dodi — Prayer welcoming the Sabbath Queen.

ma'ariv — Evening prayers.

machmir — Strict.

Mashiach — Messiah.

mechanech — Teach; teacher.

mensch — A decent person.

mefarshim — Commentators.

middah (pl. *middos*) — Character traits.

Midrash — Homiletic interpretations of Scripture by the Sages.

minhag — Custom.

minchah — Afternoon prayers.

minyan — Quorum of men, required for communal prayer.

Mishkan — Tabernacle.

mitzvah (pl. *mitzvos*) — Commandment.

mohel — One who performs a circumcision.

nachas — Pleasure.

neiro ya'ir — May his candle illuminate.

neshamah — Soul.

nussach — Style; version.

olim — Immigrants to Israel.

parashah — Weekly Torah portion.

peirush — Interpretation.

Pesach — Passover.

pikuach nefesh — A matter of life and death.

Rachmana litzlan — God forbid.

rav — Rabbi.

rechilus — Gossip.

Shabbos — Sabbath.

shacharis — Morning prayer.

shalom bayis — Marital harmony.

shemiras halashon — Guarding one's speech.

sheyibaneh bimheirah v'yameinu — It should be built speedily in our days, referring to the Holy Temple.

shidduch — Marriage prospect.

shiur (pl. *shiurim*) — Lesson.

shul — Synagogue.

simchah — Happy occasion.

sukkah — Booth.

tallis — Prayer shawl.

talmid — Student.

tamim — Pure; innocent.

teshuvah — Repentance.

Tu BiShevat — The New Year of the trees.

tza'ar gidul banim — The difficulty of raising children.

tzaddik (pl. *tzaddikim*) — Righteous person.

tzedakah — Charity.

tznius — Modesty.

V'nishmartem l'nafshoseichem — You shall guard your lives.

zechus avos — Merit of the fathers.

zeide — Grandfather.

Suggested Reading

his and the following list are by no means exhaustive. Although there are many books on parenting, some of which repeat the same ideas (this one included), it is worth reading them because sometimes the same idea presented in a different way makes a stronger impression.

While reading, listening to tapes, and prayer are all wonderful means of perfecting one's parenting *middos*, when the case calls for it, don't hesitate to seek guidance from a qualified professional, be it a *rav*, a counselor, or an experienced educator.

Abramov, Tehilla. *Straight from the Heart: A Torah Perspective on Mothering through Nursing.* Targum Press.

Abramov, Rabbi Yirmiyohu, and Tehilla Abramov. *Our Family, Our Strength: Creating a Jewish Home.* Targum Press.

Adahan, Miriam. *Awareness.* Feldheim Publishers.

Adahan, Miriam. *Appreciating People.* Feldheim Publishers.

Adahan, Miriam. *Raising Children to Care: A Jewish Guide to Child-Rearing.* Feldheim Publishers.

Briggs, Dorothy Corkille. *Your Child's Self-Esteem.* Doubleday, 1975.

Covey, Stephen R. *The 7 Habits of Highly Effective Families.* Simon and Schuster, 1997.

Eisemann, Moshe M. *Of Parents and Penguins.* Feldheim Publishers.

Faber, Adele, and Elaine Mazlish. *How to Talk So Kids Will Listen and Listen So Kids Will Talk.* New York: Avon Books, 1980.

Faber, Adele, and Elaine Mazlish. *Siblings without Rivalry.* New York: Avon Books, 1987.

Feinhandler, Rabbi Yisroel Pesach. *Beloved Children: Insights on Raising Children from the Weekly Parashah.* Feldheim Publishers.

Gans, Rabbi Moshe. *Make Me, Don't Break Me: Motivating Children for Success at Home and in the Classroom.* Mesorah Publications.

Hirsch, Rabbi Shamshon Raphael. *Yesodos HaChinuch.* Netzach.

Keleman, Rabbi Lawrence. *To Kindle a Soul: Ancient Wisdom for Modern Parents and Teachers.* Targum Press/Leviathan Press.

Leach, Penelope. *Your Baby and Child: From Birth to Age Five.* Revised edition. Knopf, 1997.

Levi, Miriam. *More Effective Jewish Parenting.* Mesorah Publications.

Orlowek, Rabbi Noach. *My Child, My Disciple.* Feldheim Publishers.

Orlowek, Rabbi Noach. *Raising Roses among the Thorns: Bringing Up Spiritually Healthy Children in Today's Society.* Feldheim Publishers.

Radcliffe, Sara Chana. *The Delicate Balance: Love and Authority in Torah Parenting.* Targum Press.

Schwartz, Rabbi Yoel. *The Eternal Jewish Home: A Torah Perspec-

tive on Raising Children. The Jerusalem Academy of Jewish Studies/Yeshivat Dvar Yerushalayim.

Shulman, Avi. *Criticizing Children: A Parent's Guide to Helping Children*. Feldheim Publishers.

Twerski, Rabbi Abraham J., M.D. *I Didn't Ask to Be in This Family*. Henry Holt Publishers.

Twerski, Rabbi Abraham J., M.D., and Ursula Schwartz, Ph. D. *Positive Parenting: Developing Your Child's Potential*. Mesorah Publications.

Wagschal, Rabbi S. *Successful Chinuch: A Guide for Parents and Educators*. Feldheim Publishers.

Walder, Chaim. Kids Speak series. Feldheim Publishers.

Wikler, Dr. Meir. *Partners with Hashem*. ArtScroll.

Wolbe, Rabbi Shlomo. *Planting and Building: Raising a Jewish Child*. Translated by Rabbi Leib Kelemen. Feldheim Publishers.

Suggested Listening

Tapes on parenting by:

Rabbi Paysach J. Krohn

Rebbetzin Tzippora Heller

Rabbi Yaakov Shapiro

Dr. Miriam Adahan

Rabbi Dr. Mordechai Glick series entitled "Raising Happy Children in an Unhappy World"

Rabbi Akiva Tatz

Rabbi Zev Leff

In Hebrew:

Rabbi Yechiel Yaakovson

Rabbi Emmanuel Tehilla

These tapes are available through *gemachim* or for purchase from Aish HaTorah or the lecturers themselves.